Hydroponic HANDBOOK

How Hydroponic Growing Systems Work

J. Benton Jones, Jr.

GroSystems, Inc.
Anderson, South Carolina

2011

GroSystems, Inc.
109 Concord Road
Anderson, South Carolina 29621

© 2011 by GroSystems, Inc.

Jones, J. Benton, Jr.

Hydroponic HANDBOOK: How Hydroponic Growing Systems Work

ISBN – 978-1456557072

Table of Contents

Table of Contents, con't

Preface

This treatise describes the basic principles of hydroponics applied to growing plants in various configurations, with or without a rooting medium, and with the use of various nutrient solution formulations. Sufficient information is provided in order for the reader to understand how these hydroponic growing systems work, with enough detail to understand how the parameters that define their application and use parameters work together in a hydroponic growing system. In addition, the basic principles of plant nutrition, elemental forms and root function are briefly discussed as they apply to the various methods of hydroponic growing of plants.

.

A. Abbreviations

In order to make the text easier to read, appropriate commonly used abbreviations are used, except when there could be confusion or a misunderstanding when an abbreviation is used in some contexts. The following are the abbreviations used in the text for elements, compounds, ionic forms, and units of measure.

Elements and their Symbols

Element	Symbol	Element	Symbol
Boron	B	Molybdenum	Mo
Calcium	Ca	Nickel	Ni
Carbon	C	Oxygen	O
Chlorine	Cl	Phosphorus	P
Copper	Cu	Potassium	K
Fluoride	F	Silicon	Si
Hydrogen	H	Sodium	Na
Iron	Fe	Vanadium	V
Magnesium	Mg	Zinc	Zn
Manganese	Mn		

Compounds	Elemental Formula
Ammonia	NH_3
Ammonium molybdate	$(NH_4)_6Mo_7O_{24}\cdot4H_2O$
Ammonium nitrate	NH_4NO_3
Ammonium dihydrogen phosphate	$NH_4H_2PO_4$
Ammonium sulfate	$(NH_4)_2SO_4$
Borax	$Na_2B_4O_7\cdot10H_2O$
Boric acid	H_3BO_3

Calcium carbonate	$CaCO_3$
Carbon dioxide	CO_2
Calcium nitrate	$Ca(NO_3)_2 \cdot 4H_2O$
Calcium sulfate	$CaSO_4 \cdot 2H_2O$
Copper sulfate	$CuSO_4 \cdot 5H_2O$
Diammonium hydrogen phosphate	$(NH_4)_2HPO_4$
Hydrochloric acid	HCl
Ferric chloride	$FeCl_3 \cdot 6H_2O$
Ferric sulfate	$Fe_2(SO_4)_3$
Ferrous ammonium sulfate	$(NH_4)_2SO_4 \cdot FeSO_4 \cdot 6H_2O$
Ferrous sulfate	$FeSO_4 \cdot 7H_2O$
Magnesium carbonate	$MgCO_3$
Magnesium potassium sulfate	$MgSO_4 \cdot K_2SO_4 \cdot 6H_2O$
Magnesium sulfate	$MgSO_4$
Manganese chloride	$MnCl_2 \cdot 4H_2O$
Manganese sulfate	$MnSO_4 \cdot 4H_2O$
Molybdic acid	H_2MoO_4
Molybdic acid	$H_2MoO_4 \cdot H_2O$
Monoammonium phosphate	$NH_4H_2PO_4$
Nitric acid	HNO_3
Phosphoric acid	H_3PO_4
Potassium chloride	KCl
Potassium nitrate	KNO_3
Potassium sulfate	K_2SO_4
Silica	SiO_2
Silicic acid, ortho	H_4SiO_4
Sodium molybdate	Na_2MoO_4
Sodium nitrate	$NaNO_3$
Sodium silicate	$Na_2SiO_3 \cdot 4H_2O$
Solubor (sodium borate)	$H_3BO_3/Na_2B_4O_7 \cdot 5H_2O/$ $Na_2B_{10}O_{16} \cdot 10H_2O$
Sulfuric acid	H_2SO_4
Zinc sulfate	$ZnSO_4 \cdot 7H_2O$

Ionic Forms	**Elemental Forms**[Valance]
Aluminum	Al^{3+}
Ammonium	NH_4^+
Borate	$B_4O_7^{2-}$
Chloride	Cl^-
Calcium	Ca^{2+}

Copper	Cu^{2+}
Fluoride	F^-
Iron (ferrous, ferric)	Fe^{2+} and Fe^{3+}
Magnesium	Mg^{2+}
Manganese	Mn^{2+}
Molybdate	MoO_4^{2-}
Phosphate, tri-	PO_4^{3-}
dihydrogen phosphate	$H_2PO_4^-$
monohydrogen phosphate	HPO_4^{2-}
Potassium	K^+
Nickel	Ni^{2+}
Nitrate	NO_3^-
Silicate	SiO_4^{4-}
Sodium	Na^+
Sulfate	SO_4^{2-}
Vanadate	VO_4^{2-}
Zinc	Zn^{2+}

Units of Measure

Unit	Abbreviation	Unit	Abbreviation
parts per million	ppm	gram	g
liter	L	kilogram	kg
milliliter	mL	pound	lb
milligrams per liter	mg/L	ounce	oz
grams per liter	g/L	gallon	gal

B. Hydroponic Terminology
(some terms are defined based only on their application to hydroponics)

As with any subject, there develops a jargon that relates to that subject, terms that become familiar and accepted by those intimately engaged, but which may not be understood by those unfamiliar with the subject. The following are terms frequently used in reference to the subject of hydroponics.

Aeroponics: the process of growing plants in an air or mist environments without the use of soil or an aggregate medium (known as geoponics). (Source: http://en.wikipedia.org).

7

Absorption: a term used to define the uptake or passage of an ion. or water, into a plant root by crossing through a root cell membrane.

Adsorption: the attraction and adherence of a substance or ion to the surface of a plant root.

Anion: an ion in solution that has a negative charge. In chemical notation, the minus sign, indicates the number of electrons that the element will give up.

Atmospheric Demand: capacity of the air surrounding the plant to absorb water resulting in the loss of water through plant leaf surfaces, the amount depending on the temperature of the air and its relative humidity.

Availability: a term used to indicate an element that is in a form and position for root absorption.

BATO Bucket: a bucket for hydroponic use, especially designed with a small reservoir in its base and drainage nipple above the reservoir that can be attached to a PVC drainage line to carry away an overflow of nutrient solution. Available in two colors: black for cool growing conditions and beige for warm conditions (see Figure 14).

Beneficial Element: an element not essential for plants, but that, when present in a nutrient solution or rooting medium, can enhance plant growth.

Cation: an ion in solution that has a positive charge. In chemical notation, the plus sign, indicates the number of electrons that the element will accept.

Cation Exchange Capacity (CEC): the ability of a substance to hold cations on its surface by means of electrical attraction due to the fact that the substance itself, or is surface, carries a negative electrical charge.

Closed System: hydroponic system in which the nutrient solution is recovered for recirculation after solution bathes plant roots or passes through the rooting medium.

Complete Nutrient Solution: a nutrient solution that contains all of the plant-required essential mineral elements in the desired ionic form and at concentrations for ease of root absorption.

Concentrate Solution: refers to a concentrated reagent solution that is mixed with other reagent concentrates to form a nutrient solu-tion. It is common practice to give a Concentrate Solution a letter designation, such as A, B, C, etc. Another term for a Concentrate Solution is Stock Solution.

Electrical Conductivity (EC): a measure of the electrical resistance of water, a nutrient solution, or effluent from a rooting medium, indicating the concentration level of ions in solution. EC is normally expressed as milliSiemens per centimeter (mS/cm). EC can be expressed in other units: 1 dS/m = 1mS/cm = 1000 uS/cm = 1 mmho/cm.

Essential Elements: 16 elements that have been found to be necessary for a plant to grow and complete its life cycle. These elements have been divided into 3 categories: the structural elements of carbon (C), hydrogen (H) and oxygen (O); the major elements, calcium (Ca), potassium (K), magnesium Mg), nitrogen (N), phosphorus (P) and sulfur (S); and the micronutrients of boron (B), chlorine (Cl), copper (Cu), iron (Fe), manganese (Mn), molybdenum (Mo) and zinc (Zn).

Full-strength Nutrient Solution: a nutrient solution that contains all the reagents which are in the designated formulation.

Half-strength Nutrient Solution: a nutrient solution that is half the strength of the designated formulation created by diluting with water.

Hoagland/Arnon Nutrient Solutions: two formulations of reagents dissolved in water to form solutions which when applied to plant roots will supply all the plant-required essential mineral elements. This is also referred to as a Hoagland Nutrient Solution. These nutrient solutions were one of the first complete formulations published which are still in wide use.

Hydroponics (from the Greek words *hydro*, water and *ponos*, labor) is a method of growing plants using mineral nutrients solutions, in water, without soil. Terrestrial plants may be grown with their roots in the mineral nutrient solution only or in an inert medium, such as perlite, gravel, mineral wool or coconut husk (Source: http://en.wikipedia.org).

Ion: an atom or group of atoms having either a positive or negative charge from having lost or gained one or more electrons.

Feeding Cycle: the period of time when a nutrient solution is either circulated through plant roots or applied to the rooting medium.

Leachate: a solution that is obtained when a rooting medium is leached with water, the objective being to remove accumulated "salts" from the rooting medium. This solution may be considered a hazardous waste, required specialized treatment.

Leaf Analysis: a determination of the element content in a plant leaf used to evaluate the mineral element nutritional status of the plant.

Major Elements: the elements calcium (Ca), magnesium (Mg), nitrogen (N), phosphorus (P), potassium (K) and sulfur (S) essential to plants required at high concentrations (percent levels of dry weight).

Micronutrients: the elements boron (B), chlorine (Cl), copper (Cu), iron (Fe), manganese (Mn), molybdenum (Mo) and zinc (Zn) essential to plants required at low concentrations [parts per million (ppm) levels of dry weight).

Mineral Elements: a term used to identify those inorganic elements, both major elements and micronutrients, essential to plants.

Mineral Nutrition: the study of the function of the essential elements as they relate to the growth and well being of plants.

Nutrient Elements: a term used to identify those elements, both major elements and micronutrients, essential for plant growth.

Nutrient Solution: a water solution containing one or more of the essential elements in suitable form and concentration for absorption by plant roots, providing the means for supplying the plant with one, a portion or all of its required essential mineral elements.

Open System: that hydroponic system in which the nutrient solution is discarded after bathing the plant roots or passing through a rooting medium.

Passive Hydroponics: semi-hydroponics or passive sub-irrigation is a method of growing plants without soil, peat moss, or bark. Instead an inert porous medium transports water and fertilizer to the roots by capillary action (Source: http://en.wikipedia.org).

Photosynthesis: a process that converts carbon dioxide into organic compounds, especially sugars, using the energy from sunlight (Source: http://en.wikipedia.org).

Plant Analysis: a determination of the elemental content of a selected plant part used to evaluate the nutritional mineral element status of the plant.

Plant Nutrient Elements: refers to those elements essential to plants.

Plant Requirement: that quantity of an essential element required for the normal growth and development of plants without stress from a deficiency or an excess.

Raft Hydroponic Growing System: a method of growing lettuce and herbs in which the plants are floated on a pool of nutrient solution.

Recirculation: refers to the re-use of a nutrient solution, primarily related to "closed" hydroponic growing systems.

Reverse Osmosis: a method for generating pure water.

RO Water: water that has been purified by the reverse osmosis process.

Soilless Plant Growing: the growing of plants without the use of soil.

Steiner Nutrient Solution: a specifically formulated nutrient solution that contains the ions in solution in a ratio for optimum root absorption (see page 64).

Stock Solution: refers to a concentrated reagent solution that is mixed with another reagent stock solutions to form a nutrient solution. Another term for a Stock Solution is Concentrate Solution, frequently given a letter designation, A, B, C, etc.

Structural Elements: the elements carbon (C), hydrogen (H) and oxygen (O) that are combined in the photosynthesis process, form-ing carbohydrates that become the organic structure of a plant.

Sufficiency: a term used to designate that concentration of an essential element that is required for normal plant growth in either the plant itself or in the rooting medium.

Tracking: a procedure for monitoring the elemental content of a nutrient solution and/or plant tissue over time used as a means for regulating the mineral element nutritional status of both.

Transpiration: the loss of water vapor from plant leaf surfaces, the rate and extent of loss determined by the atmospheric conditions surrounding the plant (air temperature, humidity, vapor pressure deficit), root water availability, water status of the plant, stage of growth and leaf physical condition and area.

Vertical Farming: proposed agricultural techniques involving large-scale agriculture in urban high-rises or "farmscrapers," using advanced greenhouse technology and greenhouse methods, such as hydroponics. These buildings would produce fruit, vegetables, edible mushrooms and algae year-round.

(Source: http://en.wikipedia.org).

C. The Essential Elements Required by Plants

There are 16 elements that must be present in the plant at specific concentrations in order for a plant to grow and function normally, their essentiality based on the criteria established by Arnon and Stout (1939). These elements have been divided into two categories based strictly on their concentration required. In percent concentrations greater than 0.1% of the plant's dry matter are termed the *major elements*. There are 9 major elements: calcium (Ca), carbon (C), hydrogen (H), magnesium (Mg), nitrogen (N), oxygen (O), phosphorus (P), potassium (K) and sulfur (S). In concentrations less than 0.1% of the plant's dry matter are termed the *micronutrients*. There are 7 micronutrients: boron (B), chlorine (Cl), copper (Cu), iron (Fe), manganese (Mn), molybdenum (Mo) and zinc (Zn).

Three of the major elements, C, H and O, are designated by the author as the "structural elements", combined in the process called photosynthesis to form carbohydrates, compounds that constitute 90 to 95% of the dry weight of the plant. The remaining 6 major elements, Ca, K, Mg, N, P and S, constitute 5 to10% of the plant dry weight. The 7 micronutrients, B, Cl, Cu, Fe, Mn, Mo and Zn, constitute less that 1% of the plant dry weight. The essential

Table 1.	The Essential Plant Nutrient Elements Identified by Form Utilized and their Biochemical Functions	

Essential Element	Form Utilized	Biochemical Functions
C, H, O	CO_2, H_2O	combined in the photosynthesis process to form a carbohydrate when combined forms the carboneous physical structure of the plant

11

N, S	NO_3^-, NH_4^+, SO_4^{2-}	combined with carbohydrates to form a amino acids and proteins that are involv involved in enzymatic processes
P	PO_4^{3-}, $H_2PO_4^-$, HPO_4^{2-}	phosphate esters involved in energy transfer reactions
B	H_3BO_3, BO_3^{3-}	esterification with native alcohol groups; involved in carbohydrate metabolism
K, Mg, Ca, Cl	K^+, Ca^{2+}, Mg^{2+}, Cl^-	sustain the osmotic potentials, balancing anions, controlling membrane permeability and electro-potentials, associated with the quality of generated fruit, Mg is a component of the chlorophyll molecule
Cu, Fe, Mn, Zn, Mo	Cu^{2+}, Fe^{2+}/Fe^{3+}, Zn^{2+}, MoO_4^2	enables electron transport by valency change, serve as co enzymes, present predominately in a chelated form incorporated in a prosthetic group

elements, form utilized and biochemical function are given in Table 1.
For the structural elements, C, H and O, the source of C is carbon dioxide (CO_2) in the air, and H and O from plant absorbed water. The 6 major mineral elements and the 7 micronutrients must be present as an ion in the rooting medium, whether it be soil, a soilless medium, a hydroponic nutrient solution, or a nutrient solution within the rooting medium in order to be absorbed by the plant root for plant utilization. The ionic form(s) of the 6 major elements and 7 micronutrients are:

Major Elements (ionic form)	**Micronutrients (ionic form)**
Nitrogen	Boron (BO_3^{3-})
Ammonium (NH_4^+)	Chlorine (Cl^-)
Nitrate (NO_3^-)	Copper (Cu^{2+})

12

Phosphate, tri- (PO_4^{3-})

Iron (ferrous, ferric) $(Fe^{2+}$ and $Fe^{3+})$

Manganese (Mn^{2+})

  dihydrogen phosphate $(H_2PO_4^{-})$ Molybdenum (MoO_4^{2-})

  monohydrogen phosphate (HPO_4^{2-})

Potassium (K^{+})

Zinc (Zn^{2+})

Calcium (Ca^{2+})

Magnesium (Mg^{2+})

Sulfate (SO_4^{2-})

Which form of P exists in solution will depend on pH, dihydrogen phosphate $(H_2PO_4^{-})$ and/or monohydrogen phosphate (HPO_4^{2-}) in acid solutions and tri-phosphate (PO_4^{3-}) in solutions when the pH approaches neutrality (7.0).

The terminology that identifies the name of an essential element and its ionic form in solution is not consistent for all the essential elements. For the elements K, Ca, Mg, Cu, Mn and Zn, the same word is used to define both, but for the other essential elements, the elemental word and that in solution in ionic form is different. For N, the 2 ionic forms are the nitrate (NO_3^{-}) anion or the ammonium (NH_4^{+}) cation; for P, either dihydrogen phosphate $(H_2PO_4^{-})$ or monohydrogen phosphate (HPO_4^{2-}) anion; for S, the sulfate (SO_4^{2-}) anion; for B, the borate (BO_3^{3-}) anion; for Cl, the chloride (Cl^{-}) anion; for Fe, either the ferrous (Fe^{2+}) or ferric (Fe^{3+}) cation; and for Mo, the molybdate (MoO_4^{2-}) anion.

Two ions, nitrate (NO_3^{-}) and potassium (K^{+}) present in fairly high concentrations in rooting media, are readily plant absorbed, while all the other ions are selectively absorbed. All of the element ions are in one of 3 categories based on their relative ease for root absorption:

Relative Ease for Root Absorption

Easily	Moderately	Least Easily
- - - - - - - - - - - - - - - - - element (ion form) - - - - - - - - - - - - - - - - -		
Nitrogen	magnesium (Mg^{2+})	calcium (Ca^{2+})
nitrate (NO_3^{-})	sulfur (SO_4^{2-})	boron (BO_3^{3-})
ammonium (NH_4^{+})	iron (Fe^{2+}, Fe^{3+})	
phosphorus $(HPO_4^{2-}; H_2PO_4^{-})$	zinc (Zn^{2+})	
potassium (K^{+})	molybdenum (MoO_4^{2-})	
manganese (Mn^{2+})		
chlorine (Cl^{-})		

D. Beneficial Elements

Although no such category has been officially established, many believe that more than the 16 essential elements must be present in the plant to ensure vigorous growth and development. In earlier times in the hydroponic culture of plants, an A–Z solution containing 20 elements was added to the nutrient solution containing the essential elements known at that time. The idea was to ensure that most every element found in both soils and plants would be included in the nutrient solution. Much of the interest in these so-called "beneficial elements" may be academic as their presence in plants could be only consequential. It also may be that their presence in plants will have no affect on plant growth, unless conditions exist that would make that element a limiting factor. There is also the danger that their presence in plants may be detrimental, and therefore should be excluded from a nutrient solution rather than included.

Many of the so-called beneficial elements are common contaminates in rooting medium used for the hydroponic medium-growing methods,. Therefore, their addition to a nutrient solution formulation is not justified. Untreated water used in making a nutrient solution or for irrigating the plants may also contain these elements. Currently the only element among the identified beneficial elements that should be considered for addition to a nutrient solution formulation is Si.

Plants that are soil-grown can contain substantial quantities of Si, equal in concentration (% levels in the dry matter) to that of the other major mineral essential elements. Most of the Si absorbed [plants can readily absorb silicic acid (H_4SiO_4)] is deposited in the plant as amorphorous silica, $SiO_2 \cdot nH_2O$, known as opals.

A noted plant physiologist has identified 6 roles for Si in plants, both physiological and morphological, recommending that Si as sodium silicate (Na_2SiO_3), be included in a nutrient solution formulation at 0.25 millimoles (mM). In more recently conducted hydroponic studies, it has been shown that when the Si content in a nutrient solution is at 140 ppm, yield improvements for both lettuce and bean crops occurred. In studies with greenhouse-grown tomato and cucumber, plants were less vigorous and susceptible to fungus disease attack if Si was not included in the nutrient solution formulation. Best growth was obtained when a liter (L) of nutrient solution contained 100 mg silicic acid $(H4SiO4)$. Both sodium or potassium silicate are reagent forms of Si that have been included in nutrient solution formulations since both are water-soluble compounds, while silicic acid is only partially water-soluble.

14

There are other elements that would fall into the "beneficial" category since they have been found to have identifiable effects on the nutrition of some plants, those being the partial substitution of Na for K, and V for Mo. Both Na and V are ever-present in the environment, so adding sources of these elements to a nutrient solution would generally be of no advantage.

E. Root Function and Elemental Absorption

The passage of ions from a hydroponic nutrient solution or root medium solution into the plant root is a complex process that is not completely understood. The observed characteristics are:

- the ability of ions to move against a concentration gradient.
- the observed ability of plant roots to selectively absorb or exclude ions.

The ability of ions to move across a concentration gradient requires energy generated by root respiration. In order for respiration to occur, oxygen (O_2) is required; therefore roots must be in an aerobic environment in order to actively absorb ions.

Roots also exhibit a cation exchange capacity (CEC), as cations can be held or removed from root surfaces by this exchange process. This apparent CEC may be one of the factors that gives rise to the ability of certain cations to be absorbed by the plant root to the exclusion of others.

The physical characteristics of the root itself have an influence on ion absorption. As the root changes anatomically, function and rate of ion absorption changes. In general, as the distance from the root tip increases, the rate of ion absorption decreases. In addition, at a short distance from the root tip, root hairs may form that will significantly enhance ion uptake due to the large increase in root surface area generated. Root hair development is affected by the physical and chemical characteristics around the developing root in root medium growing systems. Root hair development is uncommon for roots growing in non-medium growing systems. In addition, the formation of lateral roots will also increase the contact surface, and in turn, enhance ion absorption. Although root surface area is an important factor in ion absorption, it is the active functioning of roots that determines the rate and extent of ion absorption. Therefore the size of a root mass does not directly correlate with its rate of root ion absorption. It has been demonstrated that just one actively functioning root can be adequate to supply the entire plant with all of its elemental requirements.

It is generally believed that a carrier system exists that literally *carries* an ion across the root cell membrane, although the specific identification of such carriers in not known. An ion is attached to a carrier, and the combined unit is transported from the outer root surface across the root cell membrane and deposited into the root itself. The ion is released and the carrier moves back across the cell membrane to repeat the process with another ion. It is believed that carriers are ionspecific, which partially explains adsorption difference observed for certain element ions, monovalent versus divalent ions. Another concept is based on an ion pump system that assists in the transport of ions across the root cell membrane. For both of these systems to work, energy is required that is derived from root respiration. This is the reason for roots requiring an aerobic (O_2 containing) atmosphere.

Water and ion absorption are thought to be related, water acting like a "carrier" for ion transfer across the root membrane. To some degree, this is true, but it is not the primary mechanism for ion absorption as described above. If water absorption, however, is impaired for extensive periods of time, particularly during critical periods such as fruit bearing, fruit yield and quality can be impaired, and for the plant itself, nutrient element stress can occur. The same root environment conditions for water absorption must exist as that for ion absorption; an aerobic (O_2 containing) atmosphere.

Chapter I. Historical Background

The technique for growing plants in an element-rich, aerated water solution had its debut in the mid-1850s. Researchers devised this technique as a means for determining those elements when absent from the root-bathing solution, plant growth would be significantly impaired, followed by the death of the plant. Today researchers are still using this same technique as a means of growing plants that allows the user to easily modify the elemental content of the solution (called the *nutrient solution*) bathing the roots of the plant.

The word "hydroponics" was first used by Dr. W. F. Gericke who published an article in the February 1937 issue of the scientific journal, *Science* 178:1, an article that described a method for growing plants without the use of soil. Hydroponics was initially devised by Dr. W.A. Setchell, a faculty member at the University of California, who combined two Greek words, "hydro" meaning water, and "ponics" meaning work, therefore giving the meaning "working water" for the growing of plants without the use of soil. In a series of articles in the early 1930s, hydroponics was hailed as the "future" for the large scale production of food plants by eliminating the need for soil. Due to the economic conditions of that period, followed by WWII, focus was shifted away from this grand idea temporarily.

During WWII, the United States Army established hydroponic gardens on several islands in the Pacific in order to supply troops operating in that area with fresh vegetables. In gravel beds using the flood-and-drain method, tomato and lettuce were grown hydroponically. Following WWII, similarly designed hydroponic farms were established, mainly in semi-tropical and tropical areas of the world, for the commercial production of tomato and cucumber. High production costs coupled with the inability to control root diseases, however caused most of these enterprises to fail. The book by Eastwood (1947) reviews this era of hydroponic activity.

Today, the commercialization of hydroponics continues to attract the attention of entrepreneurs, devising systems for growing plants, such as tomato, cucumber, pepper, lettuce, strawberry, flowers, etc. (mainly high cash value crops), in various configurations using environmentally controlled greenhouse structures, and also to a limited degree, also in outdoor settings. Hydroponic growing systems are still being devised and refined, striving to improve plant performance and achieve economic soundness.

Chapter II. Hydroponic Operating Systems

A hydroponic operating system is defined by how a nutrient solution is used. There are 2 types:
- an "open" system in which the nutrient solution is passed just one time through the plant root mass or rooting medium, and then discarded.
- a "closed" system in which the nutrient solution, after passing through the plant root mass or rooting medium, is recovered for reuse.

Both techniques can be applied to all hydroponic growing systems. The "open" system can be wasteful of water and reagents depending on how the root mass or rooting medium pass-through is conducted. A nutrient solution can be formulated by injecting a nutrient-containing reagent concentrate (sometimes referred to as a Stock Solution) into a flowing stream of water, therefore not requiring a storage vessel for a formulated nutrient solution. This system has the advantage that the roots are being exposed to a constant composition nutrient solution. Since a nutrient solution after passing through the plant root mass or rooting medium can be defined as a potential "hazardous waste," therefore requiring recovery and specialized treatment before being disposed.

With the "closed" system, there must be a means for recovering the nutrient solution after passing through the plant root mass or rooting medium. There are several options on how the recovered nutrient solution is treated before its reuse, circulation back through the plant root mass or rooting medium. Normally, the nutrient solution is brought back to its original volume by adding water, and then re-circulating without further treatment. Alternatively, pH and nutrient element contents can be determined and adjusted to bring both back to their original levels. Lastly, treatment can be done to remove by filtering suspended materials, and/or sterilizing by ozone injection or ultraviolet (UV) exposure, and/or aerating (adding oxygen) by bubbling air or O_2 gas through it. Without these treatments, there is the possibility for the occurrence of plant nutrient element insufficiencies and plant root disease incidence. Depending on how the recovered nutrient solution is treated, its may be possible to continuously use it over the entire growth period of the plant being grown hydroponically.

Chapter III. Hydroponic Growing Systems

There are basically 6 hydroponic growing systems, each having their own unique establishment and supporting requirements, and operating characteristics. Some systems can be operated manually; others require electrically-driven pumps, timers, and special equipment in order to deliver the nutrient solution to and through the plant root mass or rooting medium.

Section 1. Systems Without a Rooting Medium

There are 3 hydroponic growing systems that do not require a rooting medium: standing-aerated/circulated nutrient solution, nutrient film technique (NFT) and aeroponics. The advantage of these methods is that whatever effects may occur with the use of a rooting medium are not factors. These three hydroponic growing methods have limited commercial application for their use with particular crops.

a. Standing-Aerated/Circulated Nutrient Solution

The roots of the plant are suspended in a container filled with a nutrient solution that is being continuously aerated. An illustration of this method is shown in *Figure 1*.

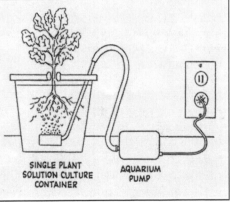

SINGLE PLANT SOLUTION CULTURE CONTAINER   AQUARIUM PUMP

Figure 1

The standing-aerated nutrient solution technique was devised by researchers in the mid 1800s as a method to determine and verify the essentiality of those elements suspected to be required by plants for growth and life cycle completion (see pages 11-13). With this method researchers were able to remove from the nutrient solution all traces of the element being investigated. They did not have to deal with another source of that element that could be introduced as a constituent in a rooting media. The last element to be determined as essential using the standing-aerated nutrient solution technique was Cl in 1954, a significant chemical and analytical accomplishment since Cl is ever-present in the environment as well as the fact that the plant requirement for Cl is very low. This method is still in wide use today for plant nutritional research studies and for growing plants when there are particular nutritional characteristics required.

The size of the rooting vessel must be sufficient to accommodate the roots without being bunched together forming anaerobic pockets. The 2 important factors are the size of the vessel in terns of root accommodation, as well as the volume of nutrient solution it holds, The greater the volume, the lesser the influencing effect on nutrient solution composition, and the less frequent the nutrient solution will require modification or replacement.

This hydroponic method has been generally considered not suited for the commercial production of plants. However, more recently it has found an application, sometimes referred to as a "raft system," for the production of lettuce and herbs. A flat shallow water-tight container is filled with nutrient solution, forming a pond, and a raft is then placed upon that pond. The most frequently used raft material is Styrofoam, as it is inexpensive and also is a durable substance that can be either discarded when the crop is harvested or reused after sterilization. A rockwool cube or small cup of rooting media containing a germinated lettuce or herb seedling is placed into spaced openings made in the sheet with the plant roots suspended in the nutrient solution. The nutrient solution is kept aerated by constant movement under the floating sheet. In some designs, air lines are placed in the bottom of the pond, bubbling air up through the nutrient solution in order to maintain the desired oxygen (O_2) level in the nutrient solution, while also keeping the nutrient solution stirred. The major factor determining the volume of nutrient solution is its depth, which must be sufficient so that replacement and/or pH and elemental composition modification are not required between the time of placement of the seedlings and crop harvest. Water additions or a modified nutrient solution formulation will normally be required, however, in order to maintain the initial depth of nutrient solution. The suggested depth of nutrient solution is between 4-5", but it can be as much as 10" as depth is also important for minimizing temperature fluctuations under changing environmental conditions. Lettuce being grown using

Figure 2

this hydroponic system is shown in **Figure 2**.

The system can be used outdoors when rainfall events are infrequent and/or are of low amounts for any one event.

This method for growing lettuce and herbs is well-suited for use by the home gardener by using a large child's plastic swimming pool. A sheet of Styrofoam is cut to fit the diameter of the swimming pool. Small openings are cut in the Styrofoam sheet for the placement of lettuce or herb seedlings that have been germinated in either rockwool cubes (recommended due to their stability) or cups of rooting medium. The swimming pool is filled with nutrient solution and the Styrofoam sheet placed on the surface of the nutrient solution as shown in **Figure 3**. Each day the edge of the floating sheet should be lifted in order to stir the nutrient solution and keep it aerated. Water, or a specialized

Figure 3

nutrient solution formulation for maintaining constancy in nutrient solution composition, will need to be added in order to maintain a constant depth of solution.

Required Equipment: water tight rooting container; stirring and/or aeration system in the nutrient solution rooting vessel or pool; for the raft method, Styrofoam sheets or other suitable material.

Advantages:
- System is easy to assemble and operate.
- Method is fairly efficient in its use of water and reagents to formulate the nutrient solution.
- For the raft system, the nutrient solution-holding pool can be constructed using plastic sheeting as the liner of varying dimensions and depth with minimum requirements for pumps, piping, and storage containers.

21

- The plastic sheeting used to form the nutrient solution pool can be either discarded after use, or cleaned and sterilized for the next crop.
- A child's plastic swimming pool can be used by the home gardener as the nutrient solution container.
- For raft material, a Styrofoam sheet is most suitable, an inexpensive and durable substance that can be either discarded when the crop is harvested, or reused after sterilization.
- This system can be used outdoors when rainfall events are infrequent and/or of low amounts for any one event.

Disadvantages:
- Method is limited to the growing of a single plant per vessel of sufficient size to accommodate the plant roots. It requires constant aeration and periodic replacement of the nutrient solution, depending on the plant being grown and its growth rate.
- Nutrient solution composition will change with time, requiring replacement or adjustment to keep it at its original composition during the growth period of the plant.
- The raft growing system is only suitable for the production of short-stem plants and those that come to maturity is a short time period (30 to 45 days).
- Once rafts are floated onto the nutrient solution pond, depending on the size of the pond, the crop may not be easily attended until harvest. Therefore, this system is not suited for plants that require daily individual attention.
- The nutrient solution bed must be level and water tight.
- The nutrient solution requires constant aeration and/or circulation to maintain the desired oxygen (O_2) level.
- Root disease is a constant threat, for with use the nutrient solution becomes a brew for the growth of bacteria and fungi.
- Temperature control of the nutrient solution can pose a problem in environments that have widely varying air temperatures.
- Method is wasteful of water and reagents when the nutrient solution is eventually discarded, possibly requiring treatment as an environmental hazardous waste.

b. Nutrient Film Technique (NFT)

In 1975, the Nutrient Film (sometimes the word "Flow" is used instead of "Film") Technique was introduced, being known by its acronym, NFT, coined by its inventor, Allen Cooper (Cooper, 1976). With its introduction (Savage, 1985), came increased interest in the commercial production of tomato, cucumber, pepper and lettuce using this unique method, replacing the flood-and-drain method that was in common use at that time. Initially, NFT was considered a major advancement in hydroponics. With the NFT system, plants, either rooted in a rockwool cube or block of similar stable rooting medium, are set in an enclosed sloping (2 to 3% slope) trough with a nutrient solution periodically introduced at the head of the trough, that flows down the trough by gravity. The width, height and length of the trough are not set dimensions. Troughs can be made using a variety of materials: PVC gutters and pipes, plastic lined wood or metal constructed troughs, and even light-proof plastic sheeting. The material selected must be water proof, and the constructed trough must have sufficient strength to maintain its shape and be unbending.

With each irrigation, sufficient nutrient solution must be discharged at the head of the trough so that there is an outflow of the nutrient solution at the end of the trough. The volume and timing of nutrient solution introduction is based either on a set time schedule or determined by the water needs of

Figure 4

the plants. For better control of the nutritional status of the plants, some recommend applying a "concentrated" nutrient solution formulation at the beginning of each day, followed by either a "dilute" nutrient solution or water only irrigations when the plants require water. With each of these nutrient solution/water systems, separate delivery and recovery tanks are required. With recirculation of the nutrient solution, volume, pH and essential element adjustments as well as filtering to remove suspended materials and sterilization are required. Today, the NFT method is primarily used for the production of lettuce and herbs as shown in **Figure 4**. The functional design of the NFT method is illustrated in **Figure 5**.

Required Equipment: trough, nutrient solution storage tanks and end of trough collection system; electrical pumps and programmable operating system; nutrient solution compensation treatment system (see pages 50-51).

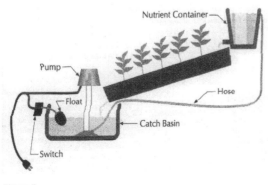

Figure 5

23

Advantages:
- The system is easy and inexpensive to set up.
- This technique is well suited for the growing of lettuce.
- Plastic sheeting can be used to construct a trough, as long as it is placed on a firm unbending surface

Disadvantages:
- Trough length and the volume of nutrient solution applied at each irrigation can be a factor affecting plant performance at the end of the trough due to changes in oxygen (O_2) and elemental content of the flowing nutrient solution.
- Retention of the applied nutrient solution in the root mass will adversely impact plant growth.
- Disease is a constant threat and may be difficult to control if occurring with long-term crops, such as tomato, cucumber and pepper.
- Tomato, cucumber and pepper plant roots can eventually fill the trough, impeding the flow of nutrient solution so that it will begin to flow over the top of the root mass, not through it.
- Anaerobic conditions can develop within the root mass, which results in root death and eventually the death of the plants.
- Flaws in NFT design and function characteristics has essentially limited its use for the growing of lettuce and herbs.

c. Aeroponics

Plant roots are suspended in an enclosed chamber, either continuously or intermittently bathed with a spray or mist of nutrient solution as is illustrated in **Figure 6**. The rooting chamber may be a box as is illustrated in Figure 6, or it can be a teepee or lean-to structure with the plants placed on openings on the slanted sides with their roots suspended in the enclosure. The roots are essentially growing in air that promotes root generation and extensive growth. Therefore, this method has been successfully used for stimulating root initiation for those plant species difficult to root from stem cuttings. Of all the hydroponic growing systems, it is the most novel, but it is limited practical application.

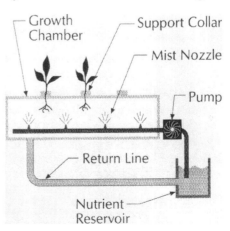

Figure 6

The method is well suited for the growing of small plants, such as lettuce and herbs, particularly for those herbs where the roots are the harvested plant part. The finer the nutrient solution droplets, the greater will be the potential for adherence on the roots. High pressure pumps are required for dispensing the nutrient solution through the spray nozzles. The nutrient solution will require filtering to remove suspended particles that can clog nozzle openings. The nutrient solution formulation must be sufficient to meet the nutritional needs of the plant since elemental root contact is intermittent. In some system designs, a shallow pool of nutrient solution is allowed to form in the bottom of the rooting chamber. A portion of the plant roots can then lay in this pool, which serves as a supply of both needed water and nutrient elements, particularly when the atmospheric demand is high. Being a "closed" system, the nutrient solution will periodically require volume, pH and nutrient element content adjustment as will as filtering and sterilization (see pages 50-51). A commercial application of this method is the AeroGarden (www.aerogarden.com).

Required Equipment: nutrient solution storage tanks; specially designed nutrient solution dispensing nozzles; high pressure pumps; filtering system to remove suspended particles in the nutrient solution; programmable operating system; nutrient solution compensation treatment system.

Advantages:

- It is easy and inexpensive to construct the root chamber which can have various designs, depending on the plant species being grown and desired outcome.
- Procedure is well suited for the growing of small plants, such as lettuce and herbs, particularly for those herbs whose roots are the primarily selected plant part.
- Method stimulates root initiation and growth, making this an excellent method for generating roots for those plant species difficult to root from stem cuttings.

Disadvantages:

- The nutrient solution must be filtered to remove suspended materials that can clog nozzle openings.
- The size of the nozzle openings will determine droplet size. The smaller the openings, the greater the pump pressure needed to discharge the nutrient solution.
- Under high atmospheric demand conditions, this system of water supply may not be sufficient to meet the plant's water needs, resulting in plant wilting.
- There is the danger of root disease occurrence due to the high atmospheric and humidity conditions within the rooting chamber.

Section 2. Systems Using a Rooting Medium

There are 3 hydroponic growing systems in this group: flood-and-drain, drip irrigation and sub-irrigation that require use of a rooting media. They are complicated in their operational characteristics due to the presence of a rooting medium whose physical, chemical and biological properties will affect root growth and function. A list of the commonly used inorganic rooting media is given in *Table 2* and organic rooting media in **Table 3.** The important

Table 2.   **Characteristics of Inorganic Hydroponic Substrates**

Substrate   **Characteristics**

Rockwool

Clean, nontoxic (can cause skin irritation), sterile, lightweight when dry, reusable, high water-holding capacity (80%), good aeration (17% air holding), no cation exchange capacity or buffering capacity, provides ideal root environment for seed germination and long-term plant growth

Vermiculite

Porous, spongelike, sterile material, lightweight, high water absorption capacity five times its own weight), easily becomes waterlogged, relatively high water-hold-ing capacity

Perlite

Siliceous, sterile, sponglike, very light, free-draining, no cation exchange capacity or buffer capacity, good germination medium when mixed with vermiculite, dust can cause respiratory irritation

Pea gravel

Particle size ranges from 5 to 15 mm in diameter, free draining. Low water-hold-ing capacity, high weight density, may require leaching and sterilization before use

Sand

Varying grain size (ideal between 0.6 to 2.5 mm in diameter), may be contaminated with clay and silt particles which must be removed, low water-holding capacity, high weight density, added to some organic mixes to add weight and improve drainage

Expanded Clay

Sterile, inert, range in pebble size to 1 and 18 mm, free draining, physical structure can allow for accumulation of water and nutrient elements, reusable if sterilized,

Pumice

Siliceous material of volcanic origin, inert, has high water-holding water capacity than sand, high air-filled porosity

Scoria

Porous, volcanic rock, fine grades used in germination mixes, lighter and tends to hold more water than sand

Polyurethane

New material which holds 75 to 80% air space and 35% water-holding capacity

Table 3.	Characteristics of Organic Hydroponic Substrates

Substrate	Characteristics

Coconut fiber

Made into fine (for seed germination) and fiber forms (coco peat, palm peat, and coir), useful in capillary systems, high ability to hold water and nutrients, can be mixed with perlite to form medium that has varying water-holding capabilities, products can vary in particle size and possible Na contamination

Peat

Used in seed raising mixes and potting media, can become waterlogged and is normally mixed with other materials to obtain varying physical and chemical properties

Composed bark

Used in potting media as a substrate for peat, available in various particle sizes, must be composted to reduce toxic materials in original pinebark (from *Pinus Radiata*), high in Mn and can affect the N status of plants when initially used, with prevent the development of root disease

Sawdust

Fresh, uncomposted sawdust of medium to course texture good for short-term uses, has reasonable water-holding capacity and aeration, easily decomposed which poses problems for long-term use, sources of sawdust can significantly affect its acceptability

Rice hulls

Lesser known and used, has properties similar to perlite, free-draining, low to moderate water- holding capacity, depending on source can contain residue chemicals, may require sterilization before use

Sphagnum moss

Common ingredient in many types of soilless media, varies considerably in physical and chemical properties depending on origin, excellent medium for seed germination use in net pots for NFT applications, high water-holding capacity and can be easily water-logged provides some degree of root disease control

Vermicast and compost

Vermicast (worm castings) and compost are used for organic hydroponic systems, varying considerably in chemical com-position and contribution to the nutrient element requirement of plants, can become water-logged, best mixed with other organically derived materials or course sand, pumice, or scoria after physical characteristics

properties associated with these substances are their inertness, water-holding capacity, ease of drainage, aeration properties (pore space), volume weight, cation exchange capacity (CEC), buffer capacity, intercellular structure, and for the organic media, their physical and chemical stability and content of plant essential and non-essential elements. In some instances, mixtures of inorganic and organic media are used to obtain certain physical and chemical properties. These properties include volume weight, ease of drainage, high air porosity, and increased cation exchange and greater water-holding capacities. Besides their physio-chemical properties, some media can be a source of essential elements or potentially toxic substances. Therefore their selection as the rooting medium or inclusion in a rooting medium mix can impact plant growth. Not all these media are suitable for use with all three of the medium-required hydroponic growing systems.

Pea gravel and course sand are the rooting media of choice for use with the flood-and-drain as well as that selected for use for the drip irrigation hydroponic growing method. Both of these substances can affect the "hydroponic" function due to the presence of impurities, both organic and inorganic. What would be considered "clean" pea gravel or course sand can be difficult to find. Water washing to remove suspended materials is required before use. In order to render both these substances "clean," however, they must be acid washed to remove extraneous materials, such as surface-adsorbed organic and inorganic substances, soil, and colloidal clay.

Other substances for use as a rooting media are being developed and marketed, some for specific use based on their unique physical and/or chemical properties, primarily inertness, and particularly water-holding capacity that allows for longer periods between nutrient solution/water irrigations.

a. Flood-and-Drain (also referred to as Ebb-and-Flow)

Beginning in the late 1930s with the commercialization of hydroponic growing, flood-and-drain was the method used for large-scale growing of vegetable crops, such as tomato, cucumber, pepper and lettuce. There are no set dimensions for the rooting bed container. It only has to be sufficient to accommodate the number of plants, provide easy access to the plants, and have a rooting medium depth sufficient to allow roots to securely anchor the growing plants.

The basic mode of operation is that a nutrient solution is pumped from a storage vessel into the base of the rooting vessel, flooding the vessel, and after several minutes, the nutrient solution flows back by gravity into the storage vessel. An illustration of the basic design for a flood-and-drain system is shown in **Figure 7**.

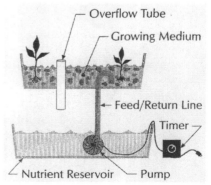

Figure 7

Clean, free from soil and/or colloidal organic and inorganic materials, pea gravel is the usual rooting media since its volume-weight is sufficient to remain in place when flooded with nutrient solution. Its water-holding capacity has two conflicting outcomes. On one hand, high retention allows for longer periods between irrigations, but on the other hand, this allows for the accumulation of "salts" and/or formation of precipitates that will, with time, adversely affect the nutritional status of the growing plants. During the growing period, the rooting medium may require periodic water leaching to remove accumulated salts. Monitoring the EC of the returning nutrient solution, or by drawing an aliquot of retained nutrient solution in the rooting medium can determine the need for water leaching.

For best plant nutritional control, a carefully crafted nutrient solution formulation is required, delivered periodically during the day. The schedule depends on an established nutritional program designed for that plant species and stage of growth, with water only irrigations when needed to maintain the plants in a turgid state. Following such a program of nutrient solution formulation and use, salt accumulation in the rooting medium can be minimized

Being a "closed" system, the nutrient solution is recirculated requiring water volume, pH and essential element concentration adjustments in order to maintain the initial volume composition. In addition, filtering removes suspended materials and sterilization, reduces the potential for root disease occurrence (see pages 50-51). Following such a routine, it is possible to use the initially formulated nutrient solution over the entire plant production cycle. However, the nutrient solution will eventually require disposal.

Today, this method of hydroponic growing is best suited for use by the home gardener due to its relatively simple design and ease of operation, as small home-type systems can be operated without the need for electrical power using gravity instead to flood and drain the rooting bed.

Required Equipment: nutrient solution storage tanks; high volume capacity pumps; programmable operating system; nutrient solution compensation treatment system.

Advantages:
- System is relatively easy to construct and operate.
- Rooting bed can vary in size based on number of plants.
- Rooting bed can be constructed using various water-resistant materials.
- The method is suitable for both large and small scale plant production

systems.
- The method is suitable for outdoor use.

Disadvantages:
- The volume weight of the rooting medium (pea gravel) requires the construction of sturdy rooting vessels and supports.
- Clean, element- and colloidal-free pea-gravel is difficult to find, and if prepared by the grower, requires the use of strong acids and acid-resistant washing facilities.
- Large rooting bed systems require high capacity pumps to quickly move the nutrient solution from the storage tank to flood the rooting bed.
- Timing for each irrigation requires a means for determining the water needs of the plants as well as a system for the nutrient element monitoring of the nutrient solution and plants.
- With accumulation of "salts" in the rooting medium, water leaching may be required. This can be costly in terms of both the amount of water required and having suitable means for collecting the leachate and for its proper disposal.
- System is wasteful of water and reagents when the nutrient solution is discarded. Disposal procedures are also required if designated as a "hazardous waste."
- With recirculation of the nutrient solution, volume adjustment is required. The pH and level of essential elements must be monitored to determine when adjustment is needed in order to maintain initial composition and avoid plant element insufficiencies.
- To prevent root disease occurrence, filtering to remove suspended materials and sterilization is required.
- Eventually precipitates of calcium sulfate and phosphate will form, providing another nutrient element source for plants, creating the potential for the occurrence of plant nutrient element insufficiencies.
- Precipitates are not removed from the rooting medium by water leaching.
- If the rooting medium is to be reused, removal of accumulated precipitates and root debris will require acid washing and steam sterilization.

b. Drip Irrigation
Today, drip irrigation is the most widely used commercial hydroponic method for the growing of tomato, cucumber, and pepper. This method provides for the delivery of a nutrient solution at the base of the plant, which is rooted in either bags or pots containing either an inorganic (perlite, rockwool, volcanic rook) or organic (peat, pinebark, core) media, or with the use of rockwool or coir slabs. Rockwool slabs are currently the rooting medium of choice with

core slabs replacing rockwool where disposal of used rockwool slabs is an issue. The nutrient solution is usually formulated with the use of injection pumps (*Figure 8*) injecting element-containing concentrates (see: Nutrient Solution Chapter IV) into a flow of water. The characteristics of the drip delivery system will be determined by the number of discharge points as well as the size and flow rates of drippers. *Figure 9* shows a dripper placed at the base of a plant rooted in a rockwool cube set on a rockwool slab.

Figure8

For all drip irrigation systems, the flow rate and volume of nutrient solution applied will depend on the water demand of the plants. Plant species, stage of growth, and frequency and volume of nutrient solution delivered with each irrigation are factors that will determine the elemental content of the delivered nutrient solution, requiring skill and experience in

Figure 9

order to set these factors. For better nutritional control, the nutrient solution is delivered only periodically during the day, the schedule depending on an established nutritional plant program for the plant species being grown, its stage of growth, and then only water when needed to keep the plants in a turgid state. Sufficient nutrient solution or water should be delivered with each irrigation so that there is a slight outflow at the base of the rooting vessel or slab, requiring a means to collect and dispose the effluent. The volume and rate of flow from a dripper will determine the distribution of nutrient solution and water within the rooting medium.

With time, there occurs a retention and accumulation of unused nutrient solution in the rooting medium that will require electrical conductivity (EC) monitoring. Depending on the physio-chemical characteristics of the rooting medium and plant species being grown, the rooting medium will require water leaching when the retained nutrient solution reaches a certain EC level.

Another form of this method places plants in the corners of buckets, stacked

31

Figure 10

at a 90 degree angle from each other forming a tower as shown in **Figure 10**, or the tower can be a large diameter plastic pipe with openings in the sides sufficient in size to accommodate the plant being grown (**Figure 11**). Access pockets should be spaced and of the size necessary to accommodate the plant species being grown, such as flowers, ornamental plants, lettuce, herbs, strawberries, and even tomato, pepper, and vine crops. The commonly used rooting medium is perlite. A nutrient solution is introduced at the top of the tower that flows down through the rooting medium by gravity, the volume and timing sufficient to provide the required water and essential plant elements for all the plants in each bucket that forms the tower. Usually sufficient nutrient solution and/or water is applied at the top of the tower so that with each irrigation, there is an outflow at the base of the tower. With some designs, drippers are placed at each plant position in the tower to ensure sufficiency in water and essential element availability. With both methods of nutrient solution/water delivery, the irrigation schedule, flow rate and volume must be sufficient to meet the water demand of the specific plants.

Figure 11

The outflow of nutrient solution at the base of the tower is either discarded or collected for reuse. With re-circulation of the nutrient solution, its pH and level of essential elements must be monitored to determine what adjustments and replacements are necessary to maintain its desired properties. Filtering is also required to remove suspended materials and sterilization to prevent root disease occurrence (see pages 50-51). Towers conserve space by allowing for large numbers of plants to be grown in a confined area. A commercial application of this method is the Verti-Gro (www.vertigro.com) tower system consisting of a stack of Styrofoam buckets.

Required Equipment: nutrient concentrate storage tanks; water pump; inline water-nutrient solution concentrate dispensing system; drip irrigation system consisting of dispensing lines and attached drippers

Advantages:
- The system is reliable in terms of plant performance.
- Method is fairly efficient in its use of water and reagents, even when operated as an "open" hydroponic system.

Disadvantages:
- Drippers require constant monitoring to ensure that there is a consistent flow of nutrient solution.
- Injection pumps for generating the applied nutrient solution require periodic inspection and adjustment.
- Timing schedule and volume of nutrient solution delivered can significantly affect plant growth, therefore requiring skill and experience to determine what is required to supply sufficient water and plant nutrient elements.
- Normally sufficient nutrient solution is delivered with each irrigation so that there is a slight outflow at the base of the rooting vessel or slab, requiring a means to collect and dispose the effluent.
- Elemental accumulation of retained nutrient solution in the rooting medium occurs that begins to impact the nutritional status of the plants.
- Electrical conductivity (EC) determination of either the outflow or retained nutrient solution in the rooting medium is required. Water-leaching of the rooting medium is needed when the EC exceeds a certain level.
- Water-leaching is costly in terms of the amount of water required and the collection and containment of the leachate for proper disposal.
- Eventually precipitates of calcium sulfate and phosphate will form, providing another nutrient element source for plants, creating the potential for the occurrence of plant nutrient element insufficiencies.
- Precipitates will not be removed by water leaching.
- The rooting media is normally discarded after one use.
- For tower systems where the nutrient solution is introduced at the top of the tower, the nutrient solution changes in elemental and oxygen (O_2) contents as its flows down the column. The plants at the base of the tower, therefore, grow slower, and possibly suffer from both O_2 and elemental stress.
- Towers will require periodic rotation so that all plants receive equal sunlight exposure

c. Sub-irrigation Growing System
The sub-irrigation growing system is a "total consumption" system since all of the applied water and plant nutrient elements are utilized. Therefore this

method is the most efficient in water and reagent use of all the hydroponic growing systems.

A nutrient solution and/or water is introduced at the base of the rooting medium, sufficient to maintain a constant depth (about 1 inch) of solution. Depth control is by hand and is determined by the position of an indicator float for the EarthBox (*Figure 12*) (www.earthbox.com).

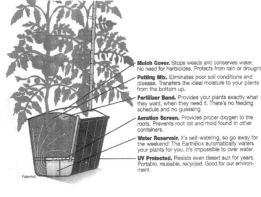

Mulch Cover. Stops weeds and conserves water. No need for herbicides. Protects from rain or drought.

Potting Mix. Eliminates poor soil conditions and disease. Transfers the ideal moisture to your plants from the bottom up.

Fertilizer Band. Provides your plants exactly what they want, when they need it. There's no feeding schedule and no guessing.

Aeration Screen. Provides proper oxygen to the roots. Prevents root rot and mold found in other containers.

Water Reservoir. It's self-watering, so go away for the weekend! The EarthBox automatically waters your plants for you. It's impossible to over water.

UV Protected. Resists even desert sun for years. Portable, reusable, recycled. Good for our environment.

Figure 12

Automatic control is obtained with the use of a float value that regulates the flow of nutrient solution or water from a reservoir into the rooting vessel as shown in *Figure 13* for the GroBox (www.hydrogrosystems.com). The AutoPot (www.autopot.com) is a commercial application of an automatic control system in which each pot has its own float value that controls the flow of nutrient solution or water from a reservoir into the base of the pot for maintaining a depth of solution.

Figure 13

The rooting medium can be either inorganic (see Table 2) or organic (see Table 3) depending on what method of plant nutrient control is used. For example, the EarthBox recommends the use of a soilless mix with all required plant nutrient elements added; therefore only water is required. For the GroBox, the rooting medium is perlite with the elemental content of the nutrient solution sufficient to meet the plant nutritional needs since all the plant nutrient elements in the nutrient solution are available for root absorption. Half-strength nutrient solution formulations have also been found to be sufficient (see page 58).

Most organic rooting media (see Table 3), except for composted milled pinebark, lack sufficient biological stability, therefore not suited for use with this hydroponic method. The rooting media must have sufficient wicking ability to maintain moist conditions to a height of 5". This allows the upper portion of the rooting medium to stay moist and yet remain aerobic, necessary conditions to keep the plant roots activity functioning. The recommended depth of the rooting medium is usually 7" above the maintained nutrient solution water table, unless the rooting media has either a higher or lower wicking property. Of all the rooting media, perlite has been found to be the best rooting medium with this method of hydroponic growing.

Experience has shown that with constant maintenance of the water table in the bottom of the rooting vessel, root development will stabilize. The roots will occupy that portion of the rooting medium where there is a balance between water and air, with the plant being in control of water and plant nutrient element absorption without being affected by the characteristics of the rooting medium.

Required Equipment: water-tight container of suitable depth; biologically stable rooting media with wicking capability; nutrient solution storage tank; means for maintaining a fixed level of nutrient solution or water in the base of the rooting medium vessel.

Advantages:
- Water and plant nutrient elements applied are completely utilized.
- System is easy and relatively inexpensive to set up.
- This system is suitable for home garden use.
- Employing a float value system of water and nutrient solution delivery, minimum attention is required.
- There is no water or nutrient solution effluent to dispose.
- There is no accumulation of elements in the rooting medium.
- With an overflow outlet installed in the rooting medium vessel, the system can be used outdoors.

Disadvantages:
- Hand-operating systems require constant monitoring of the position of the float that indicates when water or nutrient solution needs to be added to the rooting vessel.
- Depending on the rooting medium selected, its composition and/or that of the nutrient solution used, will require professional assistance to ensure that the plants receive sufficient essential nutrient elements.

Section 3. Indoor/Outdoor Environmental Considerations

Most hydroponic growing systems are designed for use in controlled environments, such as a greenhouse or growth chamber. In general, all of the hydroponic growing systems can be used outdoors depending on environmental conditions, rainfall and air temperature being major factors in determining suitability of use. Periodic heavy rainfall events can interfere with the normal functioning of all the methods except for the flood-and-drain and the tower drip irrigation methods. Excessive rain can also impact the sub-irrigation method if there is not an overflow outlet in the rooting vessel. Wide fluctuations in air temperature will have a significant effect on the NFT method. Long periods of high or low air temperatures can adversely affect the standing-aerated system using the raft system, unless there is sufficient depth of nutrient solution to buffer the effect of temperature fluctuations. With most hydroponic growing methods, constancy of the rooting environment is difficult to achieve, with the scheduling of nutrient solution and/or water delivery based on a time schedule or regulated by a determination of plant needs. These can vary with changing environmental conditions, such as air temperature, relative humidity, wind, light intensity and day length. With frequently changing environment conditions, most hydroponic growing systems may not perform well. This is a major reason why their primary use has been in controlled environments. Cost is also another determining factor where maximum performance is more likely to be achieved under controlled environmental conditions.

Chapter IV. The Nutrient Solution

Probably no other aspect of the hydroponic growing technique is as misunderstood and misused as the formulation and use of a nutrient solution. Surprisingly, most plants will grow normally under a fairly wide range of nutrient solution formulations, suggesting that plants are able to adjust to a range of elemental concentrations, ratios and varying use parameters. However, there are exceptions when the plant is growing rapidly, setting fruit, or under stress due to inadequate moisture, high or low air temperatures, or under high atmospheric demand conditions. Under such conditions, an inappropriate nutrient solution formulation and applied use parameter will affect the ability of the plant to sustain normal functions due to a plant nutrient element insufficiency. Experience may be the only judge when electing a nutrient solution formulation and associated use factors. Adjustments may have to be made to conform with the hydroponic growing system and plant species, while factoring in the environmental growing conditions.

Numerous nutrient solution formulations have been published, many found in the books authored by Barry (1996), Jones (2005) and Resh (2001), and in the book edited by Yuste and Gostincar (1999).

Section 1. Reagents

A nutrient solution is made by dissolving a weighed aliquot of a reagent or group of reagents, containing one or more of the plant essential elements, into a specified volume of water, weight and volume determined by what is the desired elemental concentration in the generated nutrient solution. The selected reagent(s) must be water soluble, free of insoluble substances and unwanted elements. In general, technical grade is the best reagent form, except for the micronutrients where reagent grade is preferred. Grade selection is a factor in terms of quality and cost. Commonly used reagents for formulating a nutrient solution are given in Table 4.

Table 4. Reagents, Formulas and Percent Elemental Content for Reagents for Making a Nutrient Solution

Reagent	Formula	Element and Percent
Major Element Sources		
Ammonium chloride	NH_4Cl	N 26
Ammonium nitrate	NH_4NO_3	N 35
Ammonium sulfate	$(NH_4)_2SO_4$	N 21.2; S 24.3

Table 4. Cont. Reagents, Formulas and Percent Elemental
Content for Reagents for Making a Nutrient Solution

Reagent	Formula	Element and Percent
Calcium nitrate	$Ca(NO_3)_2 \cdot 4H_2O$	Ca 17.0; N 11.9
Diammonium phosphate	$(NH_4)_2HPO_4$	N 21.2; P 23.5
Magnesium potassium sulfate	$MgSO_4 \cdot K_2SO_4 \cdot 6H_2O$	Mg 5.9; K 9.7; S 4.9
Monoammonium phosphate	$NH_4H_2PO_4$	N 11.8; P 26
Magnesium sulfate	$MgSO_4 \cdot 7H_2O$	Mg 9.7; S 13
Phosphoric acid	H_3PO_4	P 31
Potassium nitrate	KNO_3	K 38.7; N 13.8
Potassium sulfate	K_2SO_4	K 44.9; S 18.4

Micronutrient Sources

Reagent	Formula	Element and Percent
Ammonium molybdate	$(NH_4)_6Mo_7O_{24} \cdot 4H_2O$	Mo 53
Boric acid	H_3BO_3	B 17.5
Borax	$Na_2B_4O_{24} \cdot 10H_2O$	B 11
Copper sulfate	$CuSO_4 \cdot 5H_2O$	Cu 25.4
Iron (ferric) chloride	$FeCl_3 \cdot 6H_2O$	Fe 20.7
Iron (ferric) sulfate	$Fe_2(SO_4)_2$	Fe 14
Iron (ferrous) ammonium sulfate	$FeSO_4 \cdot (NH_4)_2SO_4 \cdot 6H_2O$	Fe 7
Iron (ferrous) sulfate	$FeSO_4$	Fe 20.1; S 11.5
Manganese chloride	$MnCl_2 \cdot 4H_2O$	Mn 27.7
Manganese sulfate	$MnSO_4 \cdot 5H_2O$	Mn 22.8
Molybdic acid	H_2MoO_4	Mo 59.2
Molybdic acid	$H_2MoO_4 \cdot H_2O$	Mo 53.3
Sodium borate (Borax)	$Na_2B_4O_7 \cdot 10H_2O$	B 11.3
Sodium molybdate	$NaMoO_4$	Mo 46.6
Zinc sulfate	$ZnSO_4 \cdot H_2O$	Zn 22.7

A nutrient solution can be made using commercial grade water-soluble
fertilizer materials, such as:

Commercial Grade Fertilizer	Elements Supplied
Ammonium nitrate	N as both ammonium and nitrate
Calcium nitrate	Ca and N (as nitrate)

Magnesium potassium sulfate (SUL-PO-MAG)	Mg, K, and S
Magnesium sulfate (Epsom Salts)	Mg and S
Monopotassium phosphate	K and P
Potassium chloride	K and Cl
Potassium nitrate	K and N (as the nitrate)
Potassium sulfate	K and S

Commercial grade fertilizers for field crop use are usually less desirable for nutrient solution formulation due to impurities, such as unwanted elements and water-insoluble substances that when in suspension will clog nozzles or drippers unless removed by filtering.

Proper identification of a reagent is essential when there exist several forms, such as potassium phosphate that exists in 2 chemical forms, as one of the following::

- potassium monohydrogen phosphate or dipotassium hydrogen phosphate (K_2HPO_4)
- potassium dihydrogen phosphate (KH_2PO_4)

This variation is due to the contents of K and P being different for these 2 compounds (see Table 4). Similar examples can be cited for boron- and iron-containing compounds, requiring knowing their chemical formula.

For those not wishing to maintain on hand the required reagents in order to make a nutrient solution, commercially prepared nutrient solution formulations are available as either nutrient element concentrates or ready-to-use formulations. It is important to know what elements and their form are in these formulations. If these formulations are marketed as a fertilizer, state law requires verified content information on the label elemental as well as form of the element. Commercially prepared nutrient solutions should provide use parameters and what the final elemental concentration in solution will be following the given preparation instructions. Formulations that contain organic substances, such as humates, chelates or growth-stimulating substances such as plant hormones should be avoided.

Section 2. Water Quality
A common recommendation is to use "pure" water for making a nutrient solution and irrigating plants. However, some substance(s) found in water may have no significant affect on plants and do not justify a search for a "pure" water source or the cost of their removal. There may be elements in a

water source that will be beneficial to plants, particularly the elements, Ca and Mg, common constituents in what is called "hard water."

Water quality is normally related to its source. Surface waters from streams, ponds and lakes may contain substances that can adversely affect plants, particularly waters that are taken from croplands. Surface runoff water from croplands can contain substances, or residues of substances, being applied to the soil, such as fertilizers and herbicides, and crop-applied pesticides. Even what is termed "ground water" from cropland areas may contain some of these same agricultural chemicals.

Constituents found in well water will reflect what exists in the aquifer. Water drawn from a limestone aquifer contain Ca and Mg, while water drawn from a granite aquifer tends to be relatively free from elemental contents. Shallow well water may contain a wide variety of elements and substances, and when anaerobic conditions exist the bicarbonate (HCO_3^-) anion, and when combined with organic materials, the sulfide (S^-) anion. Rain water will contain elements and other substances that may be suspended in the atmosphere as well as substances that have been air deposited on the collecting surfaces.

Domestic drinking water is generally suitable for use in making a nutrient solution or for irrigating plants, the only concern being the presence of fluoride (F) when F-sensitive plants are being grown.

Organic and inorganic constituents found in natural waters that could significantly affect plants must be removed if used for making a nutrient solution as well as for irrigating plants. Reverse osmosis, referred by its acronym RO, effectively removes all dissolved substances found in water. Passing water through an "activated" carbon filter will remove organic constituents, but not inorganic constituents. Passing water through an ion exchange device will remove most dissolved inorganic constituents, but the ion released in the exchange will be found in the generated water. For example, using a sodium (Na)-based ion exchange system will add the Na^+ cation to the generated water, its concentration depending on the concentration of the ions found in the original water exchanged.

Water quality parameters for making a nutrient solution or irrigating plants are given in Table 5.

Table 5. Characteristics and Elemental Content of Water Suitable for Use When Making a Nutrient Solution and Irrigating Plants

Characteristics:
pH – 5.0 to 7.0
Electrical Conductivity (EC) = <1mmho/cm;
Alkalinity ($CaCO_3$/L) = 100 ppm (2 meq/L)

Elemental Content (ppm, < less than)

Major Cations:			Major Anions		
Calcium (Ca)	- <	120	Nitrate (NO_3-N)	- <	2
Magnesium (Mg)	- <	24	Chloride (Cl)	- <	20
Potassium (K)	- <	10	Fluoride (F)	- <	0.75
Sodium (Na)	- <	50	Sulfate (SO_4)	- <	90
Ammonium (NH_4)	- <	8	Phosphate (PO_4)	- <	3
			Bicarbonate (HCO_3)	- <	122

Trace Elements:

Aluminum (Al)	- <	5
Iron (Fe)	- <	4
Manganese (Mn)	- <	1
Zinc (Zn)	- <	0.3
Copper (Cu)	- <	0.2
Boron (B)	- <	0.05
Molybdenum (Mo)	- <	0.001

Section 3. Nutrient Solution Constituent Verification

Since weighing and volume errors are easily made when making a nutrient solution, the final constituted nutrient solution should be assayed, determining its pH, electrical conductivity (EC), and element contents and their concentration. The pH and EC can be easily determined with simple instrumentation, but a laboratory analysis is required to determine the elemental concentration for a majority of the elements in a constituted nutrient solution. Today, there are devices that can be placed in the nutrient solution delivery stream that will monitor pH, EC and some of the major elements concentrations in real time (see Chapter VII). When the nutrient solution is formulated by injection of elemental concentrates into a flowing water stream, an assay of the final formulation requires verification of its elemental content as injector devices can be out of adjustment or even fail.

Weight and volume values can be confusing as there is no consistent measurement system with a mix of metric and English units used for making a nutrient solution. Conversion values are given in Chapter V, on page 54.

Section 4. Formulations

To be a "complete" nutrient solution, it must contain all of the 13 essential mineral plant nutrient elements. The major elements N, P, K, Ca, Mg and S are all required at relatively high concentration; plus the micronutrients, B, Cl, Cu, Fe, Mn, Mo and Zn, elements required at lower concentrations. When not a "complete" nutrient solution formulation, it may include only one essential element or any number of the 13 essential elements. An essential element concentration may be less than what the formulation calls for as the rooting medium may already contain that element. Also the water used for making the nutrient solution and/or used for irrigation may have a quantity of that element sufficient to meet a significant portion of that required in the formulation.

The bases for most hydroponic nutrient solution formulas are derived from the two formula (one with and the other without NH_4) published by Hoagland and Arnon (1950), the reagent list and preparation instructions given in Table 6. What most do not know is that these 2 formulations have a use component: one gallon of nutrient solution per plant with replacement on a weekly basis. If anyone of these parameters is altered, *i.e.,* the volume of solution, number of plants, and/or frequency of replacement, plant performance can be significantly affected, a factor that probably isn't fully understood or considered by those who recommend a particular nutrient solution formulation.

Table 6. Reagents and Quantity for Making a Hoagland/Arnon Nutrient Solution	
Solution No. 1	
Reagents	**to use, mL/L**
1M potassium dihydrogen phosphate (KH_2PO_4)	1.0
1M potassium nitrate (KNO_3)	5.0
1M calcium nitrate [$Ca(NO_3)_2\cdot4H_2O$]	5.0
1M magnesium sulfate ($MgSO_4\cdot7H_2O$)	2.0
Solution No. 2 (with ammonium)	
Reagents	
1M ammonium dihydrogen phosphate ($NH_4H_2PO_4$)	1.0
1M potassium nitrate (KNO_3)	6.0

Table 6. Cont. Reagents and Quantity for Making a Hoagland /Arnon Nutrient Solution	
1M calcium nitrate [Ca(NO$_3$)$_2$·4H$_2$O]	4.0
1M magnesium sulfate (MgSO$_4$·7H$_2$O)	2.0

1M = one molecular weight of the reagent

Micronutrient Stock Solution

Reagents	**mg/L**
Boric acid (H$_3$BO$_3$)	2.86
Manganese chloride (MnCl$_2$·4H$_2$O)	1.81
Zinc sulfate (ZnSO$_4$·5H$_2$O)	0.22
Copper sulfate (CuSO$_4$.5H$_2$O)	0.08
Molybdic acid (H$_2$MoO$_4$·H$_2$O)	0.02

To prepare: dissolve all the reagents in 1 liter of water.
To use: 1 mL **Micronutrient Stock Solution** per 1 liter of nutrient solution

Iron
For Solution No. 1: 0.5% iron ammonium sulfate
[FeSO$_4$·(NH$_4$)$_2$SO$_4$·6H$_2$O]
   to use: 1 mL/L nutrient solution

For Solution No. 2: 0.5% iron chelate
   to use: 2 mL/L nutrient solution

Source: *The Water-Culture Method for Growing Plants without Soil.* Circular 347. Agricultural Experiment Station, University of California, Berkeley, CA. 1950.

Commercially prepared nutrient solution formulations are readily available, either in concentrated form or prepared ready for use, either designed for universal use or for a particular growing system and/or plant species. Some formulations are for use at a particular stage of growth as the plant advances through its life cycle from seedling stage to early and mid maturity, and then to flowering and fruit formation. The need for a growth-related nutrient solution formulation is questionable when factors, such as frequency and volume applied, and nutrient solution retention and elemental accumulation in the rooting medium are significant influencing factors that affect elemental availability and plant nutritional status.

Plant specific requirements can be a factor that would justify some of the variations that exists among commonly recommended nutrient solution formulations. Not all of the essential elements have significant plant requirement aspects, but the major elements, N, Mg and P, and the micronutrients Cu, Fe, Mo and Zn, do have specific requirements for some plant species. In addition, plant requirements change with each stage of plant development, from the vegetative to fruiting stages, a factor that could justify modifying a particular nutrient solution formulation and its use factors.

Plants can respond, favorably or unfavorably, to the concentration of an element, or the ratio among elements, in a nutrient solution. In general, most nutrient solution formulations contain more P than that required by the plant which can lead to an insufficiency occurring for the elements Fe and Zn. Most nutrient solution formulations contain insufficient Mg that can lead to its deficiency in plants that have a high Mg requirement. The ratio among the major cations, K^+, Ca^{2+} and Mg^{2+}, may not be in the proper balance, and the concentration of N may be excessive when either the NO_3^- anion or the NH_4^+ cation, as well as the ratio between them, is not in the desired ratio balance.

Based on published nutrient solution formulations, the elemental concentration range for elements in solution should fall within the ranges given in Table 7 and for the Hoagland/Amon (1950) formulations, the elemental concentrations in solution are given in Table 8.

Table 7. Major Element and Micronutrient Ionic Forms and Normal Concentration Range Found in Most Nutrient Solution Formulations

Element	Ionic Form	Concentration Range
		mg/L (ppm)[a]
Major Elements		
Nitrogen (N)		
nitrate	NO_3-N	70-200
ammonium	NH_4-N	15-30
Phosphorus (P) [b]	HPO_4^{2-}, $H_2PO_4^-$	15 to 30
Potassium (K)	K^+	100 to 200
Calcium (Ca)	Ca^{2+}	200 to 300
Magnesium (Mg)	Mg^{2+}	30 to 80
Sulfur (S)	SO_4^{2-}	70 to 150

Table 7. Cont. Major Element and Micronutrient Ionic Forms and Normal Conerntration Range Found in Most Ntrient Solution Formulations

Element	Ionic Form	Concentration Range
Micronutrients		
Boron (B) [c]	BO_3^{3-}	0.10 to 0.6
Chlorine (Cl)	Cl^-	not specified
Copper (Cu)	Cu^{2+}	0.01 to 0.10
Iron (Fe) [d]	Fe^{3+}, Fe^{2+}	2 to 12
Manganese (Mn)	Mn^{2+}	0.5 to 2.0
Molybdenum (Mo)	MoO_4^-	0.05 to 0.15
Zinc (Zn)	Zn^{2+}	0.1 to 0.50

[a]Concentration range based on what is found in current literature
[b]Ionic form depends on the pH of the nutrient solution
[c]The molecule boric acid (H_3BO_3) can be absorbed by plant roots
[d]Ionic form depends on the pH and O_2 level in the nutrient solution

Table 8. Elemental Concentration in the Hoagland/Arnon Nutrient Solution Formulations

Nutrient Element	Solution No. 1	Solution No. 2
	- - - - - - - - - - ppm - - - - - - - - - -	
Nitrogen (NO_3-N)	242	220
Nitrogen (NH_4-N)	----	12.6
Phosphorus (P)	31	24
Potassium (K)	232	230
Calcium (Ca)	224	179
Magnesium (Mg)	49	49
Sulfur (S)	113	113
Boron (B)	0.45	0.45
Copper (Cu)	0.02	0.02
Iron (Fe)	7.0	7.0
Manganese (Mn)	0.50	0.50
Molybdenum (Mo)	0.010	0.010
Zinc (Zn)	0.48	0.48

A common means for formulating a nutrient solution is to prepare concentrates containing compatible elements to form what are called "stock solutions," frequently letter designated, such as A, B and C, etc., mixing only those reagents that are compatible to avoid the formation of precipitates. Aliquots of these stock solutions are then mixed with water to obtain the desired elemental concentration in the final nutrient solution. The method that mechanizes the formation of a nutrient solution is with the use of an injector pump (Figure 8) that injects a measured aliquot of stock solution into a flowing water stream. In addition, if pH correction is required, selected acids, such as concentrated sulfuric (H_2SO_4), phosphoric (H_3PO_4) or nitric (HNO_3) acids can be also injected into the same flowing water stream.

There are numerous nutrient solution formulations with widely varying elemental contents and concentrations. A number of nutrient solution formulations, representing both historical as well as those for universal use and associated with a particular hydroponic growing system and/or plant species, are given in Chapter V.

Section 5. Use of Chelates

The use of chelated forms of the micronutrients, Cu, Mn, Fe and Zn, but particularly for Fe, is a questionable practice. Being in a chelated form will not ensure "availability," but may actually interfere with root absorption and plant utilization.

It has been found that the chelate, ethylenediaminetetraacetic acid (EDTA), can be toxic to plants, and therefore some formulations use another chelate, diaminetriaminetetraacetic acid (DTPA), not thought to be plant toxic. Although chelated forms for the micronutrients have proven of value based on certain soil conditions, particularly in alkaline and organic soils and organic soilless rooting media, their use in hydroponic nutrient solutions is not justified in terms of improved availability. When adding a chelate to a mix of elements in solution, the stability of the initial chelate will depend on the concentration of the other ions in solution as well as the solution pH, which in turn, can significantly reduce the "chelate effect," therefore losing the benefit of the chelated form of the element which was the basis for its selection.

In addition, chelated forms of the micronutrients are expensive and their elemental content varies with each product. Nutrient solution formulations that use a chelated form for a micronutrient or all micronutrients may not specifically identify the actual chelated product and its micronutrient content. This lack of adequate product identification may not adversely impact the plant in terms of the micronutrient concentration in the final nutrient solution formulation; however it may lead to either an application of more or less than what is needed.

There are inorganic Fe-containing reagents that will keep Fe in solution; therefore they are available in a form able to meet the Fe requirement of the plant, such as:

- iron (ferrous) sulfate $(FeSO_4 \cdot 7H_2O)$
- iron (ferric) sulfate $[Fe_2(SO_4)_3]$
- iron (ferric) chloride $(FeCl \cdot 6H_2O)$
- iron (ferrous) ammonium sulfate $[(NH_4)_2SO_4 \cdot FeSO_4 \cdot 6H_2O]$

Section 6. Elemental Contents, Concentrations and Ratios

Element ions in a nutrient solution (see page 42) interact among themselves, exhibiting both antagonistic as well as synergistic characteristics. For example, among the major cations, K^+, Ca^{2+} and Mg^{2+}, the least com-petitive is Mg^{2+}; therefore its deficiency is likely to occur with the use of some nutrient solution formulations having high concentrations of K^+ and/or Ca^{2+} when growing Mg-sensitive plants, such as tomato. The ammonium (NH_4^+) cation is a strong competitor and can reduce the uptake of both Ca and Mg, resulting in a deficiency of either element for those plant species sensitive to either Ca or Mg, or both, For example, a high concentration of NH_4^+ in a nutrient solution when fruit is being set can result in a high incidence of blossom-end rot (BER) in tomato and pepper fruits. Therefore, some recommend that NH_4 not be included in the nutrient solution formulation during the plant's fruiting period.

There is considerable research that indicates that the form of N supplied to the plant can affect vegetative growth and fruit yield as well as related quality factors. The presence of a low concentration of NH_4-N in a nutrient solution will enhance the uptake of NO_3-N. Therefore, a mixture of NH_4-N and NO_3-N in solution frequently results in better overall plant growth. Experience suggests that at least 5-10 percent of the total N in the formulation be in the NH_4 form, even when growing tomato and pepper.

There is a synergistic relationship between nitrate-N $(NO_3$-N$)$ and K, the presence of high concentrations of NO_3-N in solution enhancing the uptake of K. The absorption of the NO_3^- anion will enhance the absorption of the K^+ cation, and to a lesser degree the Ca^{2+} and Mg^{2+} cations.

A high concentration of either cationic forms of iron (Fe^{2+} or Fe^{3+}) in solution will inhibit the absorption of Zn. In a high P-content nutrient solution, the absorption of Zn will be inhibited, and to a limited extent, it will have the same inhibiting effect on both Fe cations (Fe^{2+} and Fe^{3+}) as well as the Cu^{2+} cation. On the other hand, P in solution tends to enhance the adsorption of the Mn^{2+} cation.

As the total elemental concentration in the nutrient solution increases, the effect of the ratio of elements in the nutrient solution on the nutritional status of the plant significantly changes. For example, the ratio between or among the elements N and S, Ca and Mg, K to Ca and Mg, Fe and Zn, and K and Fe may be more important than the concentration of any one element alone. Making this observation, Steiner (1984) formulated a nutrient solution designed to minimize this effect by balancing the concentration of anions and cations in the nutrient solution. A possible solution to counter this effect is to use dilute nutrient solution formulations as is used for the sub-irrigation growing technique (see pages 57-58), thereby minimizing the need to specifically balance the anions and cations. Two Australian researches discovered the same thing when they were able to successfully grow plants hydroponically in very dilute nutrient solution formulations with plant roots suspended in a rapidly flowing, constantly maintained elemental content nutrient solution.

Section 7. Use Factors
The use of a nutrient solution has five premises:

1. mineral element concentration
2. volume applied at each irrigation
3. frequency of application
4. number of plants per volume of nutrient solution applied
5. environmental conditions

These 5 factors are interdependent, factors that vary considerably depending on the hydroponic system used and the plant requirements for each of the 6 hydroponic growing methods (see Chapter III). For example, when using the flood-and-drain hydroponic growing technique (see page 28), referred to as a "closed" system since the nutrient solution is recovered and recirculated, the decisions to be made are: (1) volume of nutrient solution per plant, (2) frequency of flooding the rooting bed, and (3) schedule for either nutrient solution adjustment and/or replacement. These are critical factors that will influence plant performance irrespective of the initial nutrient solution elemental composition. Also, these factors will determine to what extent the accumulation of "salts" and/or precipitates will occur in the rooting medium, and the frequency of water-leaching required to remove the accumulated salts. Precipitates, however, will be not removed by water leaching.

For those hydroponic growing systems in which the nutrient solution applied by means of drip irrigation unto a rooting media (such as perlite, rockwool, coir, etc. (see page 26) is not recovered, referred to as an "open" nutrient solution delivery system, the elemental composition of the nutrient solution and frequency of application will affect the residual elemental content in the rooting media. In addition, the volume of nutrient solution applied will determine the concentration distribution of elements within the rooting media. With time, the rooting media will require water leaching in order to remove "accumulated salts," whose level can be determined by an EC measurement of either an aliquot of the effluent from the rooting media or an aliquot of retained nutrient solution drawn from an access well in the rooting media. One means for minimizing salt accumulation is to apply a sufficient volume of nutrient solution to replace what was retained from the previous application. If this practice is followed, however, some means of collecting and discarding the outflow must be provided.

There are computer programs designed for specific hydroponic/crop methods that will regulate the timing and amount of a nutrient solution applied with each irrigation, including periodic adjustments based on stage of plant growth and changing environmental conditions. Past performance and experience can be factored into these programs in order to fit local environmental conditions, for the specific hydroponic growing method, greenhouse operating parameters and the skill level of the grower.

Nutrient solution formulation use factors can be defined by plant environmental conditions that will affect the rate of plant transpiration. The rate of transpiration is primarily influenced by the atmospheric conditions surrounding the plant as well as the leaf area of the plant, and to some degree stage of growth. Water needed to keep the plant turgid is root absorbed, also drawing into the plant ions in the nutrient solution surrounding the plant roots. Those ions and their amount absorbed will depend on the characteristics of the root and ion valance state and concentration in the nutrient solution. This phenomenon suggests that those use factors associated with a particular nutrient solution formulation and hydroponic growing system cannot be firmly set. What will work under one set of environmental growing conditions may not under another. This explains, in part, why a grower may have a different experience using the same hydroponic growing method and use parameters from year to year, and why one set of parameters will not apply to the same hydroponic method/greenhouse system in another location. This also suggests that the success obtained with a hydroponic growing system may be determined by how the growing system and nutrient solution use factors are adjusted to conform to the existing environmental growing conditions, such as radiant (light) energy intensity, day length, air temperature, and relative humidity. This also means that the parameters given a grower regarding how best to utilize his hydroponic/nutrient solution configuration will not equally apply to every growing situation.

Section 8. Other Factors
Filtering the nutrient solution to remove suspended particles is necessary when using the aeroponic (see page 24) and drip irrigation (see page 30) growing systems in order to prevent the clogging of nozzles and drippers, respectively.

The temperature of the applied nutrient solution can significantly affect plant growth. The rule of thumb is to maintain the nutrient solution temperature at the same temperature as the air surrounding the aerial portion of the plant. If the nutrient solution is cooler, plant wilting is likely to occur, and if higher than the ambient temperature, physiological root functions, particularly for exposed roots (aeroponics), will be impaired, affecting the absorption of water and some of the essential elements.

Root absorption of ions from a nutrient solution requires energy generated by root respiration. For absorption to occur, the roots must be in an aerobic atmosphere; that is, O_2 must be present. With some hydroponic growing systems, particularly ebb-and-flow, NFT, and when the applied nutrient solution must flow down an extended column of rooting medium, the lack of O_2 during flooding and at the end of a flow of nutrient solution, may restrict water and ion absorption. This restriction of absorption can slow plant growth and may even result in plant nutrient element insufficiencies. Therefore, preventing possible anaerobic conditions from developing around roots and/ or within the rooting environment is essential.

The lack of O_2 in the rooting environment is a major cause for root death. To ensure that a nutrient solution is air or O_2 saturated, some recommend the bubbling of either air or O_2 through the nutrient solution before re-circulating.

Section 9. Reconstitution and Treatment
For closed hydroponic systems (see page 18) due to the removal of elements from the nutrient solution by root absorption as well as by retention within the

rooting media, the recovered nutrient solution will be significantly different in its elemental composition, pH and EC from that originally applied. Bringing the nutrient solution back to its original volume by adding water and then recirculating without further treatment is a common practice. Adjusting the pH, and based on an EC determination, adding an aliquot of what is called a "topping up" nutrient solution (see page 23) is the next step in reconstituting the recovered nutrient solution. With the use of specific-ion electrodes, the concentration for nitrate-nitrogen (NO_3-N) and the cations, K^+, Ca^{2+} and Mg^{2+}, in the nutrient solution can be determined. With the addition of nutrient solution concentrates, the concentration of these ions in the recovered nutrient solution can be brought back to their original level. The extent and frequency of reconstitution steps that are employed will be determined by what is needed to ensure plant nutrient element sufficiency.

Filtering a recovered nutrient solution removes suspended materials that can be the substrate for disease organisms. Sterilization by ozone injection or ultraviolet (UV) exposure will reduce the potential for plant root disease incidence. The bubbling of either air or O_2 through the nutrient solution prior to recirculation will ensure O_2 saturation.

Depending on how the recovered nutrient solution is reconstituted and treated with each recovery and before re-circulation, it is possible to continuously use a formulated nutrient solution over the entire growth period of the plant being grown.

Section 10. Nutrient Solution and Ion Retention

With each application of a nutrient solution, a portion will be retained by the root mass, as would be the case with the NFT method. Retention occurs in the rooting media as would be the case with both the flood-and-drain and drip-irrigation methods. The extent of retention occurring with the NFT method will be determined by the density of the root mass, while the retention rate for the flood-and-drain and drip irrigation methods is determined by the physio-chemical properties of the rooting media. In addition, the volume and frequency of application of a nutrient solution, as well as when water only is applied, will affect the retention rate. With each nutrient solution irrigation, the ion concentration in the retained nutrient solution will continue to increase. This ion retention can be observed by monitoring the EC of the retained solution in the rooting medium, or by determining the EC of the nutrient solution after passing through the root mass or rooting medium. Identified as accumulating "salts," and when reaching a certain EC, these accumulations in the rooting medium will require water leaching, which was discussed earlier (see page 49). Other means for minimizing ion accumulation are different for each hydroponic growing method, as was discussed in Chapter 1. Accumulating salts reduces the ability of plant roots to absorb water and the plant-required element ions from the nutrient solution. Plant wilting during periods of high atmospheric demand can occur as a result of accumulating "salts" in the root mass or rooting media.

With time, nutrient solution retention affects the nutritional status of the growing plants. Initially, the only source for the required plant nutrient elements is that in the applied nutrient solution, unless with the drip-irrigation system, the rooting media contains a portion of a particular element or elements, or in some cases all. With nutrient solution retention, the plant now has 2 sources of elements, one being applied with each nutrient solution irrigation and the other in the retained nutrient solution. With time, a third potential source of the essential plant elements begins to form, precipitates of both calcium sulfate and phosphate that in turn will either co-precipitate or entrap the elements Mg, Cu, Fe, Mn and Zn. The rate and extent of precipitate accumulation will be determined by the same factors affecting nutrient solution retention plus the extent of water absorption by the plant that has the effect of concentrating the retained nutrient solution that favors precipitate formation. At this stage, the plant now has 3 sources for most of the essential plant elements. As a result of root contact, the formed precipitates can be dissolved; the dissolved element(s) can then be root absorbed. This explains why plant nutrient element insufficiencies may occur with time, the extent of an insufficiency depending on the growing conditions. These insufficiencies become more critical when plants are rapidly growing, setting and maturing fruit, and when under atmospheric stress conditions, such as periods of high light intensities, high or low air temperatures and/or when high atmospheric demand conditions exist.

The objective for a nutrient solution management program should be to minimize the accumulation of precipitates in the rooting medium, a task that can be difficult to achieve. It requires a nutrient solution formulation that contains that concentration and balance among the nutrient elements required for the crop being grown. Experience has shown that the Hoagland/Arnon formulation as described on page 57 meets those criteria. The next requirement is to carefully regulate the frequency of irrigations and volume applied with each irrigation to minimize the accumulation of residual nutrient solution. In addition, having the ability to irrigate with water only to maintain full plant turgidity during periods of high atmospheric demand is essential.

Chapter V. Nutrient Solution Formulations

A. Introduction

Many nutrient solution formulations have been published, some for general use, for particular hydroponic growing methods, or for particular plant species and/or stages of plant growth. The reagents selected are based on their availability, suitability in terms of elemental content and water solubility.

In some instances, the reagent may be by name only, therefore not sufficient to identify since they may exist in more than one formula form. For example, potassium phosphate exists in two common compounds:

- potassium dihydrogen phosphate or monopotassium hydrogen phosphate (KH_2PO_4)
- potassium monohydrogen phosphate or dipotassium hydrogen phosphate (K_2HPO_4)

The reagent molybdic acid exists in 2 forms:

- H_2MoO_4
- $H_2MoO_4 \cdot H_2O$

The two valance forms of iron (Fe^{2+} and Fe^{3+}) can mislead the user since there is a difference between ferrous sulfate ($FeSO_4$) and ferric sulfate [$Fe_2(SO_4)_3$] in molecular weight and the different valance state forms react differently when mixed with other reagents.

As mentioned earlier (see pages 44), most nutrient solution formulations are higher in P than required by plants and inadequate in both Mg and Zn content concentration.

The ratio among the cations, K^+, Ca^{2+} and Mg^{2+}, and if ammonium (NH_4^+) is a component in a nutrient solution formulation, can result in insufficiencies of Mg as well as Ca when either Mg- and/or Ca-sensitive plant species are being grown, and/or when a plant is under stress due to high atmospheric demand and/or exposure to high light intensity.

The selection and use of chelated forms for the micronutrients was discussed earlier (see pages 46), as some nutrient solution formulations use a chelated form of Fe, while some formulations use chelated forms for the micronutrients, Cu, Mn and Zn. For most nutrient solution formulations, the sulfate form for the micronutrients, Cu, Mn and Zn, is selected. As for Fe, other forms of Fe can be substituted for a chelated form, such as:

- ferrous sulfate ($FeSO_4 \cdot 7H_2O$)

53

- ferric sulfate $[Fe_2(SO_4)_3]$
- ferric chloride $(FeCl_3 \cdot 6H_2O)$
- ferrous ammonium sulfate $[(NH_4)_2SO_4 \cdot FeSO_4 \cdot 6H_2O]$

with no loss of Fe availability.

Application parameters should be based on use factors as was discussed Chapter IV, Section 7. In general, with frequent and/or large volumes of nutrient solution applied per plant, the elemental content of the nutrient solution should be diluted. Under such conditions, the incidence of plant nutrient element insufficiencies are more likely to occur, coupled with the possibility of a significant accumulation of retained elements and/or precipitates in either the root mass or rooting media.

The nutrient solution formulations given in this chapter are examples based on their historical aspect, universal application, use with a particular hydroponic growing method, hydroponic growing method for a particular plant species, and for use at each stage of plant growth. Included are several specialized formulations and a solid mix formulation.

B. Weight and Volume Conversions

The units of measure for nutrient solution formulations are not consistent, a mix of both metric and English units. In order to assist those having to use either of the 2 measurement systems, the following weight and volume conversions will be helpful:

Weight	
1.0 pound (lb)	= 16 ounces (oz)
1.0 pound (lb)	= 454 grams (g)
2.2 pounds (lbs)	= 1 kilogram (kg)
1.0 gram (g)	= 1,000 milligrams (mg)
Volume	
1.0 gallon (gal)	= 3.78 liters (L)
1.0 gallon (gal)	= 128 ounces (oz)
1.0 gallon (gal)	= 3,780 ounces (oz)
1.0 liter (L)	= 1,000 milliliters (mL)
1.0 milligrams/liter (mg/L)	= 1 part per million
1.0 gallon (gal) water	= 8.3 pounds (lbs)

In the preparation of a nutrient solution, the weight of each reagent is to be dissolved in a definite volume of water. For concentrate preparation, the weight of a reagent, or group of reagents, is to be dissolved in a definite volume of water, and then a specified volume of concentrate is added to a definite volume of water to form the nutrient solution.

Caution: Exercise care when reviewing these nutrient solution formulations as there is no consistent use of weights and volumes, since the formulations are given as described in the literature.

C. Historical Formulation

Knop was one of the early researchers engaged in determining the plant essentiality of elements using the hydroponic growing technique. In 1860, Knop and van Sachs were credited as being the discoverers of plant essentiality for the elements K, Ca, Mg and Fe, and then in 1865 for the element S. The essential plant elements known today as the micronutrients were yet to be identified, therefore Knop's Nutrient Solution contains only those elements identified as essential at that time.

Knop's Solution

Reagents	g/L
Calcium nitrate [$Ca(NO_3)_2 \cdot 4H_2O$]	0.8
Magnesium sulfate ($MgSO_4 \cdot 7H_2O$)	0.2
Potassium dihydrogen phosphate (KH_2PO_4)	0.2
Potassium nitrate (KNO_3)	0.2
Ferric phosphate ($FePO_4$)	0.1

D. General Purpose Formulations

Some nutrient solutions formulations are not specified for use with a particular hydroponic method and/or plant specie. The first 3 formulations, including the Hoagland/Arnon formulations, prepare multielement concentrates (sometimes referred to as Stock Solutions, and usually given a letter designation) that are then combined to form the nutrient solution. Concentrates (Stock Solutions) lend themselves for use with injector pumps (Figure 8), pumps that inject a specific quantity of concentrate into a flowing stream of water to form the nutrient solution. This method of nutrient solution formulation is primarily for use with open hydroponic growing systems.

Preparation of a Basic Nutrient Solution

To prepare the nutrient solution: mix 5 mL *Concentrate A* and 2 mL *Concentrate B* in 1 liter (L) of water.

Concentrate A	g per 10 L
Reagents	
Monoammonum phosphate ($NH_4H_2PO_4$)	340
Calcium nitrate [$Ca(NO_3)_2 \cdot 4H_2O$]	2,080
Potassium nitrate (KNO_3)	1,100
Concentrate B	
Reagents	
Magnesium sulfate ($MgSO_4 \cdot 7H_2O$	492
Boric acid (H_3BO_3)	6.2
Copper sulfate ($CuSO_4 \cdot 5H_2O$)	0.48
Zinc sulfate ($ZnSO_4 \cdot 7H_2O$)	1.20
Ammonium molybdate [$(NH_4)_6Mo_7O_{24} \cdot 4H_2O$]	0.02
Iron chelate (EDTA)	0.46

Preparation of a General Purpose Nutrient Solution using Two Stock Solutions

Stock Solution A	for 50 gallons	for 10 liters
Reagents		
Potassium nitrate (KNO_3)	1 lbs	503 g
Potassium dihydrogen phosphate (KH_2PO_4)	12 lbs	288 g
Magnesium sulfate ($MgSO_4 \cdot 7H_2O$)	21 lbs	503 g
Boric acid (H_3BO_3)	54.0 g	2.80 g
Copper sulfate ($CuSO_4 \cdot 5H_2O$)	1.0 g	0.05 g
Manganese sulfate ($MnSO_4 \cdot 4H_2O$)	28.0 g	1.50 g
Molybdic acid ($H_2MoO_4 \cdot H_2O$)	0.5 g	0.03 g
Zinc sulfate ($ZnSO_4 \cdot 7H_2O$)	4.0 g	0.20 g
Stock Solution B		
Reagents		
Calcium nitrate [$Ca(NO_3)_2 \cdot 4H_2O$]	45 lbs	1,079 g
Iron EDDHA (6% Fe)	2 lbs	48 g

To prepare the nutrient solution: dilute **Stock Solution A** and **B** at a ratio of 1 part to 200 parts (2 quarts of each stock solution in 100 gallons of water).

- -

Hoagland/Arnon Nutrient Solutions

Major Element Solution No. 1 (without ammonium)

Reagents	g/L	to use: mL/L
Potassium dihydrogen phosphate (KH$_2$PO$_4$)	136	1.0
Potassium nitrate (KNO$_3$)	101	5.0
Calcium nitrate [Ca(NO$_3$)$_2$·4H$_2$O]	236	5.0
Magnesium sulfate (MgSO$_4$·7H$_2$O)	246	2.0

Major Element Solution No. 2 (with ammonium)

Reagents		
Ammonium dihydrogen phosphate (NH$_4$H$_2$PO$_4$)	115	1.0
Potassium nitrate (KNO$_3$)	101	5.0
Calcium nitrate [Ca(NO$_3$)$_2$·4H$_2$O]	236	5.0
Magnesium sulfate (MgSO$_4$·7H$_2$O)	246	2.0

To prepare: weigh the designated amount of reagent into its own 1 liter (L) of water

To prepare the nutrient solution: add the aliquot (mL) designated for each reagent into 1 liter (L) of water to formulate the nutrient solution.

Micronutrient Stock Solution	g/L
Reagents	
Boric acid (H$_3$BO$_3$)	2.86
Manganese chloride (MnCl$_2$·4H$_2$O)	1.81
Zinc sulfate (ZnSO$_4$·5H$_2$O)	0.22
Copper sulfate (CuSO$_4$.5H$_2$O)	0.08
Molybdic acid (H$_2$MoO$_4$·H$_2$O)	0.02

To prepare: weigh all the reagents into 1 liter (L) of water. Add 1 mL concentrated nitric acid (HNO$_3$) and warm to assist in dissolving all the reagents.

To prepare the nutrient solution: add 1 mL **Micronutrient Stock Solution** into 1 liter (L) of nutrient solution.

Additional Comments: The author when using these 2 formulations found that the P level is too high, and therefore the aliquot should be 0.5 mL/L rather than 1.0 mL/L for the P-containing reagents. For the Mg-containing reagent, increase the aliquot to 3.0 mL/L from 2 mL/L.

For the **Micronutrient Stock Solution**, increase the g/L of zinc sulfate $(ZnSO_4 \cdot 5H_2O)$ to 0.44 g/L.

To utilize the synergistic effect that ammonium (NH_4) has on the root absorption of N as the nitrate (NO_3^-) anion, add one teaspoon of either ammonium nitrate (NH_4NO_3) or ammonium sulfate $[(NH_4)_2SO_4]$ to the potassium nitrate (KNO_3) reagent in the **Major Element Solution No. 1** formulation.

Dilution for use with the sub-irrigation hydroponic method: add each of the designated mL of the **Major Element Stock Solution No. 1** (without ammonium) and the **Micronutrient Stock Solution** into 1 gallon of water.

- -

In this formulation, all of the reagents are dissolved in 1,000 L of water to form a complete nutrient solution. The procedure can be cumbersome when large volumes of nutrient solution are needed.

Theoretically Ideal General Purpose Complete Nutrient Solution

Reagents	g/1,000 L
Calcium nitrate $[Ca(NO_3)_2 \cdot 4H_2O]$	1,003
Magnesium sulfate $(MgSO_4 \cdot 7H_2O)$	513
Potassium dihydrogen phosphate (KH_2PO_4)	263
Potassium nitrate (KNO_3)	583
Boric acid (H_3BO_3)	1.70
Copper sulfate $(CuSO_4 \cdot 5H_2O)$	0.39
Manganese sulfate $(MnSO_4 \cdot 4H_2O)$	6.10
Ammonium molybdate $[(NH_4)_6Mo_7O_{24} \cdot 4H_2O)]$	0.37
Zinc sulfate $(ZnSO_4 \cdot 7H_2O)$	0.30

- -

There are circumstances when formulating a nutrient solution, that one or only several of the major elements are needed. Stock solutions containing one or 2 of the major elements: N, P, K, Ca, Mg and S, can be useful when formulating a nutrient solution when a particular elemental content/concentration is required, or for reconstituting a nutrient solution that is to be recirculated when only one element or a group of elements are needed.

General Purpose Major Element Stock Solutions

Major Element Stock Solutions	g/L	to use: mL/L
Reagents		
Calcium nitrate [Ca(NO$_3$)$_2$·4H$_2$O]	787	1.25
Magnesium sulfate (MgSO$_4$·7H$_2$O)	329	1.5
Potassium dihydrogen phosphate (KH$_2$PO$_4$)	91	3.0
Potassium nitrate (KNO$_3$)	169	3.9

To prepare: dissolve each reagent in its own 1 L of water.

To prepare the nutrient solution: add the designated **to use** aliquot to 1 L of water.

- -

A micronutrient formulation for general purpose use can be useful when formulating a nutrient solution, or when reconstituting a nutrient solution that is to be recirculated by only adding the micronutrients that have been depleted.

General Purpose Micronutrient Stock Solution

Micronutrient Stock Solution	g/L
Reagents	
Boric acid (H$_3$BO$_3$)	1.23
Copper sulfate (CuSO$_4$·5H$_2$O)	0.17
Manganese sulfate (MnSO$_4$·4H$_2$O)	1.50
Ammonium molybdate [(NH$_4$)$_6$Mo$_7$O$_{24}$·4H$_2$O)]	0.06
Zinc sulfate (ZnSO$_4$·7H$_2$O)	0.38

To prepare: dissolve all the reagents in 1 liter (L) of water

To use: add 1 mL of the prepared **Micronutrient Stock Solution** to 1 liter (L) of a major element nutrient solution, or to a nutrient solution that is to be recirculated to restore its the micronutrient concentration.

- -

E. Nutrient Solution Formulations for Specific Uses

Some nutrient solution formulations are specified for use with a particular hydroponic method and/or plant specie.

Cooper's Complete Nutrient Solution Formulation for the Nutrient Film Technique (NFT) Hydroponic Growing Method

Stock Solution A

Reagents	g/45 L
Calcium nitrate [Ca(NO$_3$)$_2$·4H$_2$O]	10,030
Fe EDTA	790

Stock Solution B

Reagents	
Magnesium sulfate (MgSO$_4$·7H$_2$O)	5,130
Potassium dihydrogen phosphate (KH$_2$PO$_4$)	2,630
Potassium nitrate (KNO$_3$)	5,830
Boric acid (H$_3$BO$_3$)	17
Copper sulfate (CuSO$_4$·5H$_2$O)	3.9
Manganese sulfate (MnSO$_4$·4H$_2$O)	61.0
Ammonium molybdate [(NH$_4$)$_6$Mo$_7$O$_{24}$·4H$_2$O)]	3.0
Zinc sulfate (ZnSO$_4$·7H$_2$O)	4.4

To prepare the nutrient solution: add 4.5 L **Stock Solution A** and 4.5 L **Stock Solution B** to 1,000 liters of water

- -

Nutrient Solution Formulation for Growing Cucumber Using Drip-Irrigation Hydroponic Method

Stock Solution A	kg/1,000 L
Reagents	
Calcium nitrate [Ca(NO$_3$)$_2$·4H$_2$O]	44.4
Potassium nitrate (KNO$_3$)	62.7
Ammonium nitrate (NH$_4$NO$_3$)	5.0

Stock Solution B
Reagents

Potassium dihydrogen phosphate (KH_2PO_4)	22.0
Magnesium sulfate ($MgSO_4 \cdot 7H_2O$)	50.0

Micronutrient Nutrient Solution	**g/1,000 L**
Boric acid (H_3BO_3)	90.0
Copper sulfate ($CuSO_4 \cdot 5H_2O$)	30.0
Manganese sulfate ($MnSO_4 \cdot 4H_2O$)	150.0
Zinc sulfate ($ZnSO_4 \cdot 7H_2O$)	5.0
Ammonium molybdate [$(NH_4)_6Mo_7O_{24} \cdot 4H_2O$]	8.0
Iron chelate (13% Fe)	1.0

To prepare the nutrient solution: mix equal volumes of **Stock Solutions A** and **B** in water until the EC is 1.0 mS/cm.

- -

Nutrient Solution Formulations for a Particular Growing Method and Plant Species

(Hydroponic Nutrient Solution for Lettuce Grown using the Raft System)

Part A	**grams/10 liters**
Reagents	
Calcium nitrate [$Ca(NO_3)_2 \cdot 4H_2O$]	625
Potassium nitrate (KNO_3)	73
Iron chelate	50

Part B	
Reagents	
Potassium nitrate (KNO_3)	73
Potassium dihydrogen phosphate (KH_2PO_4)	99
Magnesium sulfate ($MgSO_4 \cdot 7H_2O$)	213
Boric acid (H_3BO_3)	3.9
Copper sulfate ($CuSO_4 \cdot 5H_2O$)	0.3
Manganese sulfate ($MnSO_4 \cdot 4H_2O$)	8.0
Zinc sulfate ($ZnSO_4 \cdot 7H_2O$)	1.1
Ammonium molybdate [$(NH_4)_6Mo_7O_{24} \cdot 4H_2O$]	0.1

To prepare the nutrient solution: dilute 1 part of **Part A** and **Part B** to 100 part's of water.

Final ppm in Nutrient Solution: N = 116, P = 21, K = 82, Ca = 125, Mg = 21, S = 28, Fe = 6.8, Mn = 1.98, Zn = 0.25. B = 0.70. Cu = 0.07, Mo = 0.05; EC = 1.0 mScm

Nutrient Solution Formulas for Tomato, Lettuce and Rose using Rockwool-Drip Irrigation or NFT Hydroponic Growing Methods

	Tomato	Lettuce	Rose
Major Elements			
Reagents	------ g/10 L ------		
Calcium nitrate [Ca(NO$_3$)$_2$·4H$_2$O]	680	407	543
Magnesium sulfate (MgSO$_4$·7H$_2$O)	350	404	429
Potassium chloride (KCl)	170	----	----
Potassium dihydrogen phosphate (KH$_2$PO$_4$	200	136	204
Ammonium nitrate (NH$_4$NO$_3$)	----	60	----
Micronutrients			
Reagents			
Iron chelate (10% Fe)	15	19.6	19.6
Manganese sulfate (MnSO$_4$·4H$_2$O)	1.78	960 mg	3.9
Boron (Solubor)	2.43	970 mg	1.1
Copper sulfate (CuSO$_4$·5H$_2$O)	120 mg	120 mg	120 mg
Sodium molybdate (Na$_2$MoO$_4$)	128 mg	128 mg	128 mg
Zinc sulfate (ZnSO$_4$·7H$_2$O)	280 mg	552 mg	448 mg

Note: weight for several reagents are in milligrams (mg)/10 L.

To prepare the nutrient solution: dilute 1 part of **Major Elements** and **Micronutrients** to 100 parts of water.

Nutrient Solution Formulation Adjustments based on Stage of Plant Growth for Chili Peppers

	Seedling	Young Plants	Cropping
Part A			
Reagents	-------- g/25 liters --------		
Calcium nitrate [Ca(NO$_3$)$_2$·4H$_2$O]	1,079	2,132	2,490

Potassium nitrate (KNO$_3$)	247	472	810
Calcium chloride (CaCl$_2$)	69	----	----
Iron EDTA	125	125	125

Part B
Reagents

Potassium dihydrogen phosphate (KH$_2$PO$_4$)	183	694	967
Potassium nitrate (KNO$_3$)	247	472	810
Magnesium sulfate (MgSO$_4$·7H$_2$O	303	1,225	1,842
Manganese sulfate (MnSO$_4$·4H$_2$O)	20	20	20
Boric acid (H$_3$BO$_3$)	9.7	9.7	9.7
Copper sulfate (CuSO$_4$·5H$_2$O)	0.7	0.75	0.75
Ammonium molybdate [(NH$_4$)$_2$MoO$_4$)]	0.26	0.26	0.26
Zinc sulfate (ZnSO$_4$·7H$_2$O)	2.7	2.75	2.75

To prepare the nutrient solution: add equal volumes of **Part A**
and **Part B** to 100 L of water
> **Comment:** this series of nutrient solution formulations suggest that as the chili pepper plants advance through their growth cycle, the nutrient element requirements change; therefore justifying the change in nutrient solution formulation. The NFT method is that used. No instructions are given for the irrigation schedule or quantity of nutrient solution delivered with each irrigation.

- -

F. Specialized Nutrient Solution Formulations
Some nutrient solution formulations have general use applications that only contain the micronutrients, or they have specialized use based on the balance among the elemental constituents.

Arnon's Micronutrient Formula

Reagents	mg/L
Boric acid (H$_3$BO$_3$)	0.48
Copper sulfate (CuSO$_4$·5H$_2$O)	0.008
Manganese sulfate (MnSO$_4$·H$_2$O)	0.25
Zinc sulfate (ZnSO$_4$·7H$_2$O)	0.035
Molybdic acid (MoO$_3$·2H$_2$O)	0.1104

To prepare: dissolve all reagents in 1 liter (L) of nutrient solution.

- -

Recipe for Preparing 100 Gallons of a
Steiner Nutrient Solution

Stock Solution Part 1		
Reagent	grams*	ounces
Calcium nitrate [Ca(NO$_3$)$_2$·4H$_2$O]	364.9	12.9
Stock Solution Part 2		
Reagents		
Potassium dihydrogen phosphate (KH$_2$PO$_4$)	83.1	2.9
Potassium nitrate (KNO$_3$)	55	1.9
Potassium sulfate (K$_2$SO$_4$)	177.2	6.1
Iron EDTA (13% Fe)	14.5	---
Zinc EDTA (14% Zn)	0.5	---
Copper EDTA (14.5% Cu)	0.3	---
Manganese EDTA (12% Mn)	3.1	---
Sodium molybdate (Na$_2$MoO$_4$·2H$_2$O)	0.1	---
Sodium borate (Na$_2$B$_4$O$_{74}$10H$_2$O)	3.3	---
Stock Solution Part 3		
Reagent		
Magnesium sulfate (MgSO$_4$·7H$_2$O)	193.1	6.8

*grams and/or ounces per 4 liters of water

To prepare a nutrient solution: add 1 L of each **Stock Solution** to 25
    gallons of water

Comments: Steiner's concept is to balance the cations and anions and to set
    a particular cation ratio. With the 3 cations, Ca, K and Mg, in their own
    Stock Solution, it is possible to set the ratio among the cations by varying
    the volume of Stock Solution used to formulate the nutrient solution.
- -

G. A Solid Matrix Formulation
There is significant advantage in having the reagents in solid form for making
a nutrient solution so that only a weight or volume measurement is sufficient
to make a nutrient solution.

Reagent A
Calcium nitrate [Ca(NO$_3$)$_2$·4H$_2$O]

Reagent Mix B	grams	ounces
Potassium nitrate (KNO$_3$)	2,275	80.25
Magnesium sulfate (MgSO$_4$·7H$_2$O)	1,757	62.00
Potassium dihydrogen phosphate (KH$_2$PO$_4$)	878	31.00
Boric acid (H$_3$BO$_3$)	6.0	0.200
Copper sulfate (CuSO$_4$·5H$_2$O)	2.0	0.075
Zinc sulfate (ZnSO$_4$·7H$_2$O)	1.5	0.053
Ammonium molybdate [(NH$_4$)$_6$Mo$_7$O$_{24}$·4H$_2$O]	0.35	0.0125
Iron EDTA	132.0	4.65

Preparation of Reagent Mix B: blend all the reagents together and thoroughly mix. The granular size of each reagent should be the same to ensure a homogenous mix.

To prepare the nutrient solution: to 10 liters (2.65 gallons) of water, add 1 level teaspoon of **Reagent A**, stir until dissolved, and then add 1 level teaspoon of **Reagent Mix B** and stir to dissolve.

Comment: The reagents must be of uniform particle size. To prepare a homogenous **Reagent Mix B** is not an easy task so that each teaspoon aliquot contains the weight proportion of each reagent. In addition, the mix must be stored in a moisture-free atmosphere to prevent water adsorption.

****

Chapter VI. Hydroponic Applications

Section 1. Looking Back into the Future

When the use of hydroponics was initially brought to the American public's attention in the late 1920s, there was much written as to its future, replacing soil-based growing with soilless. However, the economic conditions in the 1930s, followed by World War II, pushed this "new concept" of plant growing into the background, only to resurface following the war. Using the flood-and-drain method that had been put to use by the U.S. Army during the war years in a commercial setting proved not to be economically viable.

In the 1970s with the introduction of Dr. Allen Cooper's Nutrient Film Technique (NFT) (Cooper, 1976), there was revived interest in the commercial application of the hydroponic technique. Those searching for an alternate to the soil-growing of vegetables, *i.e.* tomato, cucumber and lettuce, in greenhouses, began to put the NFT method to use, devising various trough configurations and operating procedures. Most of these devised NFT systems did not perform well for the long-term crops, tomato and cucumber; although for the growing of lettuce and herbs, the NFT system worked quite well.

When drip irrigation was introduced as a means for delivering water to a specific spot to conserve water when irrigating field-grown crop plants, this method was adapted for delivering a nutrient solution to tomato and cucumber plants growing in various rooting media, both inorganic (Table 2) and organic (Table 3), in either pots, bags or slabs, in the greenhouse.

Since hydroponic growing is primarily being carried out in controlled greenhouse environments, the evaluation of a hydroponic application may be defined within the operating characteristics of the growing environment, such as that being done at the

Controlled Environmental Agricultural Center (CEAC) in Tucson, AZ
(http://ag.arizona.edu/ceac/).

As long as the plants are growing normally, it is assumed that the "nutrient-rich solution" (see page 42) aspect of the growing system is "working." However, little is being done to advance the "science" of the hydroponic method. Some Land-Grant Universities (Ohio State University, University of Florida, Mississippi State University, for example) are engaged in research to advance the technologic aspects of the hydroponic growing technique for use in greenhouses.

Is hydroponics a "science?" This question has been frequently asked without a definite answer. In most dictionaries, hydroponics is not defined as a science, but just another means of growing or cultivating plants. Webster's New World College Dictionary, 4th Edition (1999), however, does define hydroponics as "the science of growing or the production of plants in a nutrient-rich solution." Not even in the Wikipedia (www.wikipedia.org) description of hydroponics is the word "science" mentioned. Probably the only organization actively engaged in the science aspect is the National Aeronautic Space Administration (NASA), since some form of hydroponics will be used for growing plants in space.

Much has been written about the future of hydroponics with concerns that the limitations associated with the currently employed hydroponic techniques are not being adequately investigated and improved upon. Unfortunately, little effort is being devoted to making hydroponic growing methods more efficient in their use of water and reagents, and in turn, better meeting plant nutritional requirements.

From the time the Hoagland/Anon (see page 42) nutrient solution formulations were introduced (Hoagland and Arnon, 1950), little research has been devoted to investigating the use of these formulations under various application methodologies. It is not uncommon to read an article in a research journal or technical publication where the writer uses the term "modified Hoagland nutrient solution" without indicating whether the formulation itself was changed, or which use parameter was changed or adjusted, the original parameters being one plant per gallon of nutrient solution replaced weekly.

In the 1980s, **Hydroponic Society of America (HSA)** took the lead in gathering hydroponic enthusiasts, researchers and hydroponic commercial organizations together to exchange information, define the principles of hydroponics and advance the use of hydroponic growing techniques. HSA published proceedings of their annual meetings from 1980 to 1997, but HSA is no longer in existence. The **International Society on Soilless Culture and Hydroponics** periodically holds international conferences in various parts of the world. The magazine, *The Growing Edge*, began publication in 1980, ending in 2006, publishing articles on hydroponic topics and grower experiences.

During this time period, an industry began to emerge, providing for sale hydroponic growing systems, auxiliary equipment and nutrient solution formulations. Today this hydroponic industry is sizeable, offering a wide range of growing systems, auxiliary hydroponic equipment and supplies.

Maximum Yield is an organization that is advancing the commercialization of hydroponics by holding conferences on indoor gardening and publishing a magazine, *Maximum Yield*, a magazine that includes articles on a wide range of subjects for guiding the hydroponic grower. The magazine, *Urban Garden*, is another source for those searching for hydroponic application information.

Several commercial and educational institutions hold conferences and symposia periodically to educate the newcomer as well as provide information on hydroponic advancements and associated subjects, such as greenhouse environmental control systems, disease and insect control methods, cultural practices associated with particular crops, etc. Some of these organizations provide printed and audio materials for instructing those interested in growing hydroponically, as well as offering training programs and courses.

There are over 4.9 million hydroponic websites, making the search for reliable information difficult since many websites are not being kept current, are product oriented, or lack easy access for the searcher to make contact with the sponsor. Today, it is not the lack of information on hydroponics that is the challenge, but how one determines what information is reliable and what is not important.

Section 2. Hydroponic Research
Hydroponics is still the primary method used by those conducting plant nutritional investigations, the standing aeration method (see page 19) being the technique used since the method provides for easy precise control of the nutrient element composition of the nutrient solution.

Does the use of any of the hydroponic growing methods achieve the biological growth and/or yield potential of the plant being grown? Plants may grow well in each of the commonly used hydroponic methods, but are plants without visual symptoms of stress functioning at their maximum biological potential? Research is needed to determine what is required of a hydroponic growing system so that the hydroponic method employed is not the factor keeping the plant from achieving its genetic potential, and/or the factor contributing to the nutritional status of the plant that in turn becomes a limiting factor.

Most hydroponic growing methods are wasteful in their use of water and reagents, require the use of control devices, and have significant electrical power requirements

Section 3. Commercial Greenhouse Hydroponics

Today, in large acreage greenhouses devoted to the growing of tomato, rockwool slabs, coupled with the dispensing of a nutrient solution by means of a drip irrigation system, has become the "standard" procedure. With increasing restrictions for the disposal of rockwool slabs, coir slabs are being considered as a substitute, with studies underway to find ways to refurbish rockwool slabs after use. Much of the research and development work for this method of hydroponic growing is being supported by those in The Netherlands, who introduced the rockwool slabs/drip irrigation system and their accompanying nutrient solution formulations and use factors. Large corporate greenhouse complexes are located in The Netherlands, Canada, Mexico and the United States. In the United States, most of these complexes are located in Arizona and Colorado.

Figure 14

In a number of states in owner/operator single or 2- or 3-multibay greenhouses, tomato crops are being grown in buckets, such as the BATO bucket (*Figure 14*), or in bags of perlite, with the nutrient solution being delivered by means of a drip irrigation system (*Figure 15*). There exists an educational/supply industry providing the needed materials, including greenhouse structures and necessary control devices. Packaged greenhouse/hydroponic growing systems, including instructions for operating the hydroponic/greenhouse system, may be included, as well as offering owner-operator training and advisory services during the growing season. Some Land-Grant University Cooperative Extension Services provide instructional materials and technical support through their State Extension Specialists, the extent of services provided depending on the degree of interest and number of growers in the state. In addition, some Land-Grant Universities are engaged in applied research to advance the technologic aspects for those hydroponic growing methods in common use by either modifying or devising systems that will perform well under the regional and local climatic conditions. For most growers, their economic success is based on the availability of instructional information

Figure 15

that can be coupled with their own skills as a grower in order to produce fruit that has high market value. Research is needed to make the hydroponic methods in common use more efficient and also contribute to the biological potential of the crop being grown.

The primary challenge for these growers is their ability to select that greenhouse/hydroponic growing system that will perform under the existing and/or changing climatic conditions at their location in both cold and hot climatic regions. Production and management procedures will be different when growing into the periods of either colder or warmer climatic conditions and with increasing or decreasing light intensity and day length. Successful production will largely depend on how well the grower is able to make those adjustments that will ensure steady plant growth in order to sustain consistent yield and fruit quality production. What is missing is the ability to easily adjust the hydroponic growing method to conform to changing environmental conditions that impact plants. Water use and the absorption and utilization of the plant nutrient elements affect biological plant functions that may appear visually as a nutrient element insufficiency (primarily leaf symptoms). Poor plant performance, measured by low fruit yield and poor fruit quality (primarily small fruit) without visual plant and/or leaf symptoms, would indicate a plant nutrient element insufficiency.

Section 4. Commercial Outdoor Hydroponics
Outdoor applications of the hydroponic technique seem confined to the growing of lettuce and herbs in NFT systems, and with the use of towers (see pages 32) for the production of fruit, vegetable and flower crops, crop selection being determined by local market demands. The potential for outdoor applications is an untapped utilization of hydroponics. Without business or technical support available to the potential grower, the commercialization of outdoor hydroponics will not occur. Cost factors associated with most hydroponic growing systems, coupled with the inability to control the outdoor environment cause some to consider outdoor applications a misuse of the hydroponic growing method. Therefore, the future for outdoor applications may be slow in developing, although the potential is substantial.

Section 5. Urban Agriculture
The production of food plants in an urban setting has attracted much attention, the focus primarily on traditional systems of plant production that presently excludes hydroponics. Soil resources are usually limited and of questionable quality in urban environments, but soil-plant production is still the traditional method by those promoting urban agricultural concepts. Those investigating this subject will find a wealth of information on the

City Farmer website. Hydroponic growing systems have been incorporated into proposed large "plant growing factories," factories that have attracted architectural interest, but lack details on the hydroponic aspect of the designed system. These factories will require substantial investment capital and the hydroponic growing method selected may not be able to produce the quantity and quality of product needed to cover operating costs. The need is to devise a hydroponic growing system that is efficient in its use of water and reagents, and that will conform to the design characteristics of the structure enclosing the hydroponic system in order to maximize the productive capacity of the hydroponic method employed.

Section 6. Home Gardener (Hobby Grower)

The home gardener has few choices when selecting a hydroponic growing system that can be operated in a home garden setting due to cost and the required skill necessary to be successful. Nutrient solution formulations require a quality water supply, and the movement of the nutrient solution requires electrical power and control devices that add to both the cost and complexity of most hydroponic growing systems. With varying success, some home gardeners have devised their own hydroponic growing system based on information obtained from websites and written materials, then making decisions based on their best judgment. Presently, little is available to the home gardener in terms of a support system that would provide the necessary equipment and guidance needed to garden hydroponically.

There have been efforts to introduce simple hydroponic growing systems for use in under developed tropical and semitropical regions of the world where fresh vegetables are not readily available or they are very costly (see Institute of Simplified Hydroponics). These systems have been devised for use by individuals or small groups of individuals that have little technical training, and therefore could be utilized by the home gardener. However, even at best, most of these simple hydroponic growing systems will not produce the yield and quality that most gardeners would expect based on their soil-based gardening experience.

Section 7. Science Fair Projects

Hydroponics lends itself to demonstration projects, illustrating how a particular hydroponic growing method works as well as the ability to create visual plant effects that occur when an essential plant nutrient element is at an insufficient concentration in the rooting medium. The standing aerated nutrient solution method (see page 19) is easy to construct and operate, suitable for demonstrating the effect of changing nutrient solution composition on plant growth and visual plant appearance. For long-term studies, rooting plants in perlite, periodically irrigated with a nutrient solution, can be used to demonstrate the basic principles of the hydroponic method, growing plants without the use of soil, by varying the composition of the nutrient solution, and the frequency and volume of nutrient solution applied. The vertical growing technique (see page 32), is a unique application that can be used to illustrate the hydroponic growing technique while at the same time, creating an object of beauty when either flowers or a fruit crop such as strawberry is the test crop.

Some plants are more sensitive than others in their response to changing root environments and level of plant nutrient element availability. Depending on the objectives of the demonstration project, plant specie selection can be important. Tomato is a good "test plant" since it is responsive to nutrient element insufficiencies in terms of plant growth and visual leaf symptoms. Seedlings should be generated having access to all the required plant nutrient elements, and when the first true leaves appear, treatments should be applied that will illustrate the objectives of the project. If the project objective is to visually show the effects of an essential plant nutrient element insufficiency, a major element should be selected, such as N or P whose deficiency will easily develop visual symptoms, or either Mg or S whose deficiency symptoms are slower to develop. Due to their low plant requirement, micronutrient insufficiency symptoms are difficult to create. In addition, freeing the rooting environment of the micronutrient being studied is equally difficult.

A common error when growing plants is insufficient exposure to light, sunlight, or artificial light. A shortage of light, both in intensity and wavelength distribution, will reduce the effect of applied treatments. Supplementing daylight with artificial light is not as effective as using artificial light to extend the daylight hours.

Preparation of a nutrient solution can be a challenge depending on the resources available. Some of the reagents needed to make a nutrient solution can be found in some garden centers, and/or they may be among the reagents in a school chemistry laboratory. Unfortunately, most commercially prepared nutrient solution formulations contain most, or all, of the plant essential elements. For formulating a nutrient solution, the Hoagland/Arnon (see page 42) nutrient solution recipe is the best choice.

Section 8. Other Applications and the Future
Hydroponic food production is the only method available for use in areas of the world where soil resources are not suitable or unavailable. Hydroponic systems are in use in Antarctica (South Pole Growing Center, http://

ag.arizona.edu/ceca/) and research is being conducted for devising methods for growing plants in spacecraft and space stations, and eventually on celestial bodies. Long-term exploration of space by man will require a source of food and a means for controlling the atmospheric conditions within an enclosed environment. Hydroponically produced plant material would provide food for space workers, while providing a means for recycling human wastes. In addition, plants photosynthesize when in light, absorbing carbon dioxide (CO_2) and releasing oxygen (O_2), a process that assists in the maintenance of the balance between these two gases in the atmosphere necessary to support human activity within an enclosed environment. Providing plants with water and the required nutrient elements in a weightless environment is the challenge as well as devising an efficient recycling system that would not require having access to an outside source of water and to the essential plant nutrient elements.

Section 9. Suppliers of Hydroponic Equipment, Operating Supplies and Technical Support

CropKing, Inc., 134 West Drive, Lodi, OH 44254; 330-302-4203; www.cropking.com

HydroGardens, Inc., P.O. Box 25845, Colorado Springs, CO 80936-5845; 888-693-0578; www.hgi@hydro-gardens.com

Section 10. Current Magazines that include Hydroponic Information

Maximum Yield, Maximum Yield Publications, Inc., 2339A Delinea Place, Nanaimo, BC, Canada V9T 5L9

Urban Garden, PO Box 99, Babriola, BC, Canada VOR 1XO

Garden and Greenhouse, 6170 Forest Hills Drive, Dubuque IA 52002

Chapter VII. Hydroponic Diagnostics

For success in hydroponic growing, it's necessary to conduct assays of water, rooting media, nutrient solutions and plant tissue. Both on site and laboratory analyses will be required:

- when selecting the water source for making a nutrient solution and irrigating plants.
- for monitoring the element concentration of an initially formulated nutrient solution and that being recirculated.
- for assaying the effluent or the solution being retained in a rooting media.
- for conducting a plant analysis.

Some testing procedures can be done using relatively simple hand-held analytical devices, such as pH, electrical conductivity (EC) and Total Dissolved Solids (TDS) meters, and specific-ion electrodes for the determination of the nitrate-N (NO_3-N) anion and the K^+ cation. All these instruments are available from a number of sources, relatively easy to calibrate and use. These devices give competent results when the operating procedures and calibration requirements are carefully followed, and as long as the analytical instruments are properly maintained.

There are some assays that will require the services of a competent analytical laboratory that can be found in both the private and public sectors that have the capability and experience to perform the assays required as well as provide interpretations of the analytical results. The selected laboratory should be contacted before starting a hydroponic operation.

Water quality requirements were discussed in Chapter IV, Section 2. An assay of the selected water source is necessary to ensure that those substances present will not affect plant growth when used to formulate a nutrient solution and/or irrigate plants. Based on an assay result, it may be necessary to find another water source or to treat available water to remove unwanted substances.

When preparing a nutrient solution, weighing and volume measurement errors can be easily made; therefore there are requirements for elemental content and concentration verification. This is particularly important when a nutrient solution formulation is generated by injecting reagent concentrates (Stock Solutions) into a flowing water stream since injectors (see **Figure 8**) can easily get out of adjustment with use, or even fail.

When a nutrient solution is recirculated, its pH, EC and elemental content requires monitoring to determine its suitability for reuse as well as serving as a means for determining when reconstitution is required, and/or whether the nutrient solution should be discarded.

The retention of nutrient solution in a rooting medium results in the accumulation of what is referred to as "salts," whose increasing concentration will impede both water and elemental root absorption. These accumulations can be monitored by either assaying effluent from the rooting media, or by drawing an aliquot of retained solution from an access well in the rooting media. Normally an EC measurement is sufficient to determine when water leaching of the rooting media is needed.

Plants exhibiting abnormal leaf color and/or when either plant or leaf deformities appear, an essential plant element insufficiency may be the cause. This might require verification by means of a plant analysis. Plant essential nutrient element visual deficiency and excess symptoms are described in Table 9.

Before taking a plant tissue sample for analysis, sampling instructions should be obtained from the laboratory conducting the assay. The collection of recently matured leaf tissue from 20 to 25 plants is a common sampling recommendation. In some instances, collecting two sets of plant tissue, one set from "affected" and one from normal appearing plants can be helpful by comparison of the analytical results as a means of interpretation. A plant analysis result will verify if there is indeed a nutrient element insufficiency so that the proper corrective steps can be taken. If the plant visual symptoms are found not to be due to an essential plant nutrient element insufficiency, then another source for the cause, such as disease, insect damage or environmental stress, can be investigated.

Visually monitoring plants and the overall hydroponic operating system, frequently referred to as "walking" the greenhouse or growing area, should be done on a regular basis, even as a daily routine during critical periods of plant development, looking for inconsistencies that could lead to potential problems. Having someone not involved in the daily routine as the evaluator is desirable. When conducting a "walk through," it is important that the observer be not instructed what to look for, but be free of possible bias if given instructions. Following the "walk through," the observer and manager should focus on those observed conditions that require further investigation.

For large operations, a periodic routine for collecting and assaying nutrient solution and plant tissue should be followed with the obtained assay results then plotted over time. Based on observed changes in element content, adjustments can be made in order to prevent the occurrence of plant nutrient element insufficiencies. From such plotting results, an assessment of the observed data can be used as an input when establishing operational procedures. With the use of computer program driven operational procedures, the program can be adjusted to conform to the site growing conditions, operational characteristics of the hydroponic system used, and the operator's management skills.

Table 9. Generalized Plant Nutrient Element Deficiency and Excess Symptoms

Major Elements

Nitrogen (N)

Deficiency symptoms: light green leaf and plant color; older leaves turn yellow and will eventually turn brown and die; plant growth is slow; plants will mature early and be stunted.

Excess symptoms: plants will be dark green; new growth will be succulent; susceptible if subjected to disease, insect infestation, and drought stress; plants will easily lodge; blossom abortion and lack of fruit set will occur.

Ammonium (NH₄)

Toxicity symptoms: plants supplied with ammonium-nitrogen (NH_4-N) may exhibit ammonium toxicity symptoms with carbohydrate depletion and reduced plant growth; lesions may appear on plant stems, along with downward cupping of leaves; decay of the conductive tissues at the bases of the stems and wilting under moisture stress; blossom-end fruit rot will occur and Mg deficiency symptoms may also appear.

Phosphorus (P)

Deficiency symptoms: plant growth will be slow and stunted; older leaves will have purple coloration, particularly on the undersides.

Excess symptoms: excess symptoms will be visual signs of either Zn, Fe or Mn deficiency; high plant P content may interfere with normal Ca nutrition and typical Ca deficiency symptoms may appear.

Potassium (K)

Deficiency symptoms: edges of older leaves will appear burned, a symptom known as scorch; plants will easily lodge and be sensitive to disease infestation; fruit and seed production will be impaired and of poor quality.

Excess symptoms: plant leaves will exhibit typical Mg and possibly Ca deficiency symptoms due to cation imbalance.

Calcium (Ca)

Deficiency symptoms: growing tips of roots and leaves will turn brown and die; the edges of leaves will look ragged for the edges of emerging leaves will stick together; fruit quality will be affected and blossom-end rot will appear on fruits.

Table 9. cont'd

Excess: plant leaves may exhibit typical Mg deficiency symptoms; in cases of great excess, K deficiency may also occur.

Magnesium (Mg)
Deficiency symptoms: older leaves will be yellow, with interveinal chlorosis (yellowing between veins) symptoms; growth will be slow and some plants may be easily infested by disease.
Excess: results in a cation imbalance with possible Ca or K deficiency symptoms appearing.

Sulfur (S)
Deficiency symptoms: overall light green color of the entire plant; older leaves turn light green to yellow as the deficiency intensifies.
Excess symptoms: premature senescence of leaves may occur.

Micronutrients
Boron (B)
Deficiency symptoms: abnormal development of growing points (meristematic tissue); apical growing points eventually become stunted and die; flowers and fruits will abort; for some grain and fruit crops, yield and quality are significantly reduced; plant stems may be brittle and easily break.
Excess symptoms: leaf tips and margins turn brown and die.

Chlorine (Cl)
Deficiency symptoms: younger leaves will be chlorotic and plants will easily wilt.
Excess symptoms: premature yellowing of the lower leaves with burning of leaf margins and tips; leaf abscission will occur and plants will easily wilt.

Copper (Cu)
Deficiency symptoms: plant growth will be slow; plants will be stunted; young leaves will be distorted and growing points will die.
Excess symptoms: iron deficiency may be ·induced with very slow growth; roots may be stunted.

Iron (Fe)
Deficiency symptoms: interveinal chlorosis on emerging and young leaves with eventual bleaching of the new growth; when severe, the entire plant may turn light green.

Table 9. cont'd

Excess symptoms: bronzing of leaves with tiny brown spots, a typical symptom on some crops.

Manganese (Mn)

Deficiency symptoms: interveinal chlorosis of young leaves while the leaves and plants remain generally green; when severe, the plants will be stunted.

Excess symptoms: older leaves will show brown spots surrounded by chlorotic zones and circles.

Molybdenum (Mo)

Deficiency symptoms: symptoms are similar to those of N deficiency; older and middle leaves become chlorotic first, and in some instances, leaf margins are rolled and growth and flower formation are restricted.

Excess symptoms: not known and probably not of common occurrence.

Zinc (Zn)

Deficiency symptoms: upper leaves will show interveinal chlorosis with whitening of affected leaves; leaves may be small and distorted, forming rosettes.

Excess symptoms: iron deficiency symptoms will develop.

References*

Arnon, D.I. and P.R. Stout. 1939. The Essentiality of Certain Elements in Minute Quantity for Plants with Special Reference to Copper. *Plant Physiology* 14:371-375.

Barry, C. 1996. *Nutrients; The Handbook of Hydroponic Nutrient Solutions.* Casper Publications Pty Ltd., New South Wales, Australia.

Cooper, A. 1976. *Nutrient Film Technique for Growing Plants.* Grower Books, London, England.

Eastwood, T. 1947. *Soilless Growth of Plants.* Reinhold Publications, New York, New York.

Hoagland, D.R. and D.I. Arnon. 1950. *The Water Culture Method for Growing Plants Without Soil.* Circular 347. University of California Agricultural Experiment Station, Berkeley, California.

Jones, Jr. J. Benton. 2005. *Hydroponics: A Practical Guide for the Soilless Grower.* CRC Press, Boca Raton, Florida.

Resh, H.M. 1995. *Hydroponic Food Production,* Sixth Edition, Newconcept Press, Mahwath, New Jersey.

Savage, A.J. (ed.). 1985. *Hydroponics Worldwide: State of the Art in Soilless Crop Production.* International Center for Special Studies, Honolulu, Hawaii.

Steiner, A.A. 1984. The Universal Nutrient Solution, pp. 63-70, IN: *Proceedings Sixth International Congress of Soilless Culture,* The Hague, The Netherlands.

Yuste, Mari-Paz and Juan Gostincar (eds.). 1999. *Handbook of Agriculture.* Marcel Dekker, New York, New York.

*some of these publications can be obtained from the author

Index

Index, cont'd

Index, cont'd

About the Author

The author has written extensively on hydroponic topics and has been engaged in hydroponic research projects for much of his professional career. After obtaining a B.S. degree in Agricultural Science from the University of Illinois, he served in the U.S. Navy for two years which included a brief visit to the hydroponic gardens on the Island of Okinawa for the purchase of tomatoes and lettuce. After discharge from active duty, he entered graduate school, obtaining M.S. and Ph.D. degrees from the Pennsylvania State University in agronomy. For 10 years, Dr. Jones served as research professor at the Ohio Agricultural Research and Development Center (OARDC) at Wooster. During this time, he served on an advisory panel working with the greenhouse tomato growers located in the Cleveland, Ohio area.

Joining the University of Georgia (UGA) faculty in 1968, Dr. Jones served in various research and administrative positions. During this time, he was actively engaged in hydroponic research, advising hydroponic growers, giving talks, and writing research papers and technical articles on various aspects of the hydroponic technique. He attended all the *Hydroponic Society of America* Annual meetings, frequently serving as a speaker. He was present at that the *Hydroponics Worldwide: State of the Art in Soilless Crop Production* Conference held in Honolulu, Hawaii in 1985 when Dr. Allen Cooper and his colleagues presented papers on their newly developed Nutrient Film Technique (NFT) (see Savage, 1985). After retiring from UGA, Dr. Jones continued his hydroponic research, frequently spoke at hydroponic conferences, continued to write articles for various magazines, and briefly served as Southeastern Regional Director for CropKing, Inc.

Dr. Jones is an avid vegetable gardener, growing vegetables hydroponically in GroBoxes and GroTroughs he has developed for use in a home garden setting (www.hydrogrosystems.com).

In 1983, Dr. Jones authored his first book on hydroponics, *A Guide for the Hydroponic and Soilless Culture Grower*, with a revised addition published in 1997, titled, *Hydroponics: A Practical Guide for the Soilless Grower*, and a second edition appearing in 2005. A third edition is being prepared for publication in 2011.

Dr. Jones maintains 2 websites, www.hydrogrosystems.com and www.growtomatoes.com. He has an extensive hydroponic library, books, bulletins, research and technical papers, all editions of the *Hydroponic Society of America Proceedings*, and all issues of *The Grow-*

About the Author, cont'd

Edge magazine.

Dr. Jones is considered an authority on applied plant physiology and the use of analytical methods for assessing the nutrient element status of rooting media and plants as a means for ensuring plant nutrient element sufficiency in both soil and soilless crop production settings. At various times, he has served as a director of several university and commercial soil and plant analysis laboratories, and still serves as an advisor for 2 such laboratories.

The author can provide the reader with color prints of the figures in this book. He is available to conduct library research and other types of investigative work associated with hydroponics. The author can be contacted by mail at: GroSystems, Inc, 109 Concord Road, Anderson, SC 29621, and by email at: jbhydro@carol.net.

List of Tables

Table 1. The Elemental Plant Nutrient Elements Identified by Form Utilized and their Biochemical Functions

Table 2.   Characteristics of Inorganic Hydroponic Substrates

Table 3.   Characteristics of Organic Hydroponic Substrates

Table 4. Reagents, Formulas and Percent Elemental Content for Reagents for Making a Nutrient Solution

Table 5.   Characteristics and Elemental Content of Water Suitable for Use when Making a Nutrient Solution and Irrigating Plants

Table 6. Reagents and Quantity Required for Making a Hoagland/Arnon Nutrient Solution

Table 7.   Major Element and Micronutrient Ionic Forms and Normal Concentration Range Found in Most Nutrient Solution Formulations

Table 8. Elemental Concentrations in the Hoagland/Arnon Nutrient Solution Formulations

Table 9. Major Element and Micronutrient Visual Leaf and Plant Deficiency and Excess Symptoms

List of Figures and Captions

Figure 1. Illustration of the Standing Aerated Hydroponic Growing System (plant roots are suspended in a nutrient solution that is aerated by continuously bubbling air or oxygen into the nutrient solution)

Figure 2. Lettuce being grown in a greenhouse using the Standing-Aerated-Raft-Growing System (lettuce plants germinated in either rockwool cubes or cups of rooting medium are set in an opening in a Styrofoam sheet that is floated on a pool of nutrient solution with the plant roots suspended in the nutrient solution)

Figure 3. Lettuce being grown using the Standing-Aerated-Raft-Growing System using a child's plastic swimming pool as the nutrient solution container (lettuce plants are placed in openings in a Styrofoam sheet that is floated on the pool of nutrient solution)

Figure 4. Lettuce and herbs being grown in a NFT System (lettuce or herb plants germinated in a rockwool cube, or similar stable rooting cube, are placed on a slopping trough with nutrient solution periodically introduced at the head of the trough, flowing down the trough by gravity, supplying water and the essential elements for the growing plants)

Figure 5. An illustration of the NFT Hydroponic Growing System [nutrient solution is pumped from a storage vessel (catch basin) to head of a slopping trough, the nutrient solution flows down the trough by gravity to be collected and returned to the nutrient solution storage vesse]

Figure 6. An illustration of the Aeroponic Hydroponic Growing System. A nutrient solution is pumped from a reservoir and dispensed through nozzles located on the bottom of the rooting chamber, keeping the roots moist with a fine mist of nutrient solution. The system shown here is under the control of a microprocessor, controlling the temperature of the rooting chamber and the frequency of discharge from the spray nozzles.

List of Figures and Captions, cont'd

Figure 7. An illustration of the Flood-and-Drain Hydroponic Growing System. A nutrient solution is pumped periodically from the nutrient reservoir (sump) flooding the rooting medium. After a short period of the time, the nutrient solution drains by gravity from the growing (rooting) medium back into the nutrient reservoir.

Figure 8. Injection pumps (injection pumps vary in their capacity and operation depending on their function. Injection pumps must be initially calibrated and then monitored to ensure that their delivery rate is maintained)

Figure 9. Drippers placed at the base of tomato plants rooted in rockwool cubs placed on a rockwool slab (drippers vary in size and delivery rate, require monitoring to insure their functioning)

Figure 10. A Hydroponic Growing Tower Made of Stacked Buckets planted with lettuce. Buckets are stacked at 90 degrees angles from each other to form a column, an access hole in each bucket that allows the nutrient solution introduced at the top of the stack to flow down through the stack. The buckets are filled with a rooting medium and plants set in each bucket corner. A drip irrigation system may be used as the means for dispensing the nutrient solution, placing a dripper at each plant position. If the nutrient solution is dispensed at the top of the bucket stack, sufficient nutrient solution must be applied with each irrigation so there is an effluent at the base to be either discarded or collected for re-circulation.

Figure 11. A Hydroponic Growing Tower using a large diameter PVC pipe with openings in the pipe of sufficient size to accommodate plants (flowers are shown here). The same operating principles apply as described for Figure 10.

Figure 12. The EarthBox (the Grow Box) is a plastic container with a platform installed just above the bottom that holds the rooting medium in place above the water (or nutrient solution) reservoir. The rooting medium is either a soilless organic mix with all the required nutrient elements added, or an inorganic inert substance, such as perlite. A float indicator at one corner of the EarthBox is used to monitor the depth of the water (nutrient solution) in the bottom, used to determine when water or a nutrient solution is needed.